THE ARRIVAL OF
THE MIDLAND RAILWAY
AT KIMBOLTON, CAMBRIDGESHIRE
IN 1866

John Slack

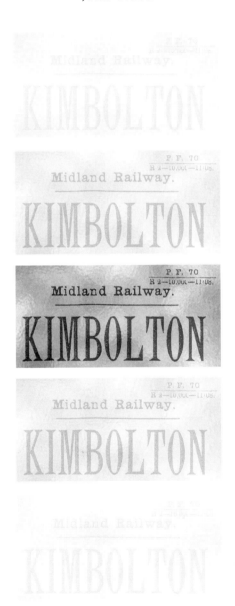

The profits from this book are to
be donated to St. Neots Museum

John Slack

THE ARRIVAL OF
THE MIDLAND RAILWAY
AT KIMBOLTON, CAMBRIDGESHIRE
IN 1866

John Slack

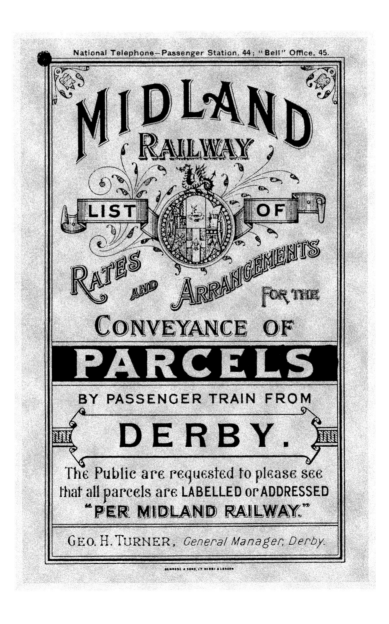

ISBN: 1 84306 051 5

British Library Cataloguing in Publication Data: a catalogue
record for this book is available from the British Library.

Printed by MPG Ltd, Bodmin, Cornwall

Design & reproduction by James Allsopp

Production by Landmark Publishing

CONTENTS

CONTENTS

ILLUSTRATIONS

ILLUSTRATIONS

ACKNOWLEDGEMENTS FOR SUPPLY OF ILLUSTRATIONS

Frontispiece & 2 - Myra Chowins

Northampton Record Office - 3, 6, 8, & 12

Dr Mike Sharman - 9

James Brunlees (great-great grandson) - 10

Brookland Cemetery Society - 11

Roy Burrows - 13

Allan Mott - 14 & 45

Peter Hall - 21 & 41 (original drawing)

Ellis & Everard plc - 22 & 23

Cockfield Women's Institute - 26

Cambridge Collection - 29

London Illustrated News - 34

Kimbolton Society - 35 & 51

St Neots Museum - 37

Raunds Historical Society - 43

St Ives Museum - 47

Huntingdon Record Office - 36, 54 & 55

Allan Sibley - 62 & 63

Midland Railway Trust - 65

Richard Casserley - 66

Bedford Record Office - St Neots Canal Survey ref. no. GA 736/1

All other illustrations are from local private collections.

Molesworth Lo.

Brington

Brithorn

Molesworth

Keyston

Great Catworth

Catworth Gorse

Leighton Gorse

Stanck Hill

Little Catworth

Leighton Bromeswold

Barham

Park W.

Alc.

Buckworth

Solow Wood

Woolley

3

Spaldwick

Upthorp

Easton

Ellington

Covington

Shire

Tilbrook

Long Stow

Ellington Thorp

Calfer W.

West W.

Under W.

Bran.

High Park F.

New Town

Lymage Wood

Graffham

Bu.

Kimbolton 63

Dudley W.

Bi.

Kimbolton Park

Stonley

Wt & Et Perry

Red Fm.

Stonley Hall

Hill F.

West W.

Diddington W.

PART OF HUNTIN

Swineshead

Dillington

Gaines Hall

Lo.

Midlow Wood

from Bedford

from Bedford

Staughton Magna

Staughton Highway

South Pa.

B E D F

Staughton Pa.

Manor House

Rushy H.

Megree

Staughton Moor

Hailweston

Weston Woods

Rookery Fm.

Hai

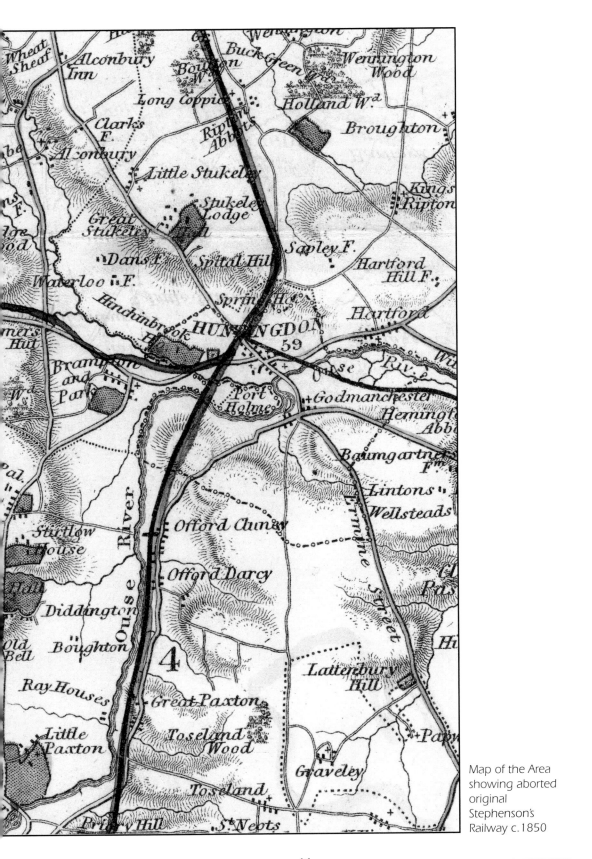

Map of the Area showing aborted original Stephenson's Railway c.1850

Setting the Scene

There are many books about railways and they can be very specialised in character. This book is an attempt to re-visit a past age, before the combustion engine, when an isolated market town and its surrounding villages were dragged suddenly out of their idyllic rural slumber with the arrival of steaming steel monsters from out of the mists.

Kimbolton is a most attractive town, originally in Huntingdonshire, but now absorbed into Cambridgeshire. It has two distinctive features. First, it has an important Tudor castle, originally with a large estate, which was the home of the Duke of Manchester until 1952, and was the home of Catherine of Aragon after her divorce from Henry the Eighth. Secondly, the town did not have any local resources of raw materials like coal, iron ore or valuable building stone as a base for heavy industry which attracted the early railways such as the Stockton & Darlington Railway.

The local Kimbolton surface geology was dominated by a film of glacial boulder clay, left behind by the melting of the Ice Age glaciers, which overlies the Oxford Clay of the Jurassic. This has had a most important influence on how local farmers coaxed a living out of the soil.

Rainfall tended to lie on the surface rather than soak away and this encouraged lush grass growth. The clay was very difficult to till until the arrival of steam ploughs, and more modern machinery, which were designed to cope with the cloying earth. The farms tended to be dominated by animal husbandry, and the opening of the railway station, albeit over two miles outside Kimbolton, must have instigated a tremendous metamorphosis on daily and seasonal farming activity.

Prior to the railway opening local farms must have relied upon their own resources for almost everything, supplemented by cartloads of expensive materials brought in along difficult muddy roads. Animals would have been driven to market by drovers and all this would have been time consuming and disruptive to efficient agricultural practice.

The Kimbolton Canal

Like many railway schemes before it, such as the Stockton & Darlington Railway, Kimbolton's was no exception and it was preceded by an embryonic canal proposal that didn't progress into any engineering activity.

In the decades before the United Kingdom's railway system began to grow there was an attempt to provide the country with an internal communications network, governed by market forces, that would improve upon the turnpike roads and be capable of handling bulkier cargoes then being generated by the Industrial Revolution.

The Grand Junction Canal had already been built, via Milton Keynes, from London to link up with the more northerly Grand Union Canal near Rugby. There were also well-established narrow-boat transport facilities on the River Great Ouse from Bedford, through St. Neots and all the way downstream to King's Lynn where the river flowed into The Wash and the North Sea.

East Anglia needed coal and iron machinery to satisfy the demands of its people and industries and east-west links were plotted by canal builders and their financial backers to bring in these materials. The scheme that was hatched to involve the Kimbolton area was devised in 1817 by the surveyor John Millington and commissioned by the Right Honourable Lord St. John (also known as Henry Beauchamp) of Bletsoe, North Bedfordshire. This settlement is a mere two miles south east of Sharnbrook near to the left bank of the River Great Ouse.

There had been an earlier attempt in 1812, to raise capital for a waterway and to be called the Bedford Canal, which would have been cut from Woughton, Milton Keynes to Bedford and on, via Sandy, to Cambridge to link up with the London & Cambridge Canal.

The Bedford scheme failed because, although the Act was passed, the London & Cambridge plan had only the southern half built thus leaving the proposed network incomplete. In addition, not enough capital was raised for the Bedford Canal scheme after the publication of the 1812 prospectus despite being backed by the heavyweights the Duke of Bedford, his son the Marquis of Tavistock, Francis Pym and Samuel Whitbread.

Fig 1 - The Proposed Newport Pagnell - Kimbolton - St Neots Canal Route

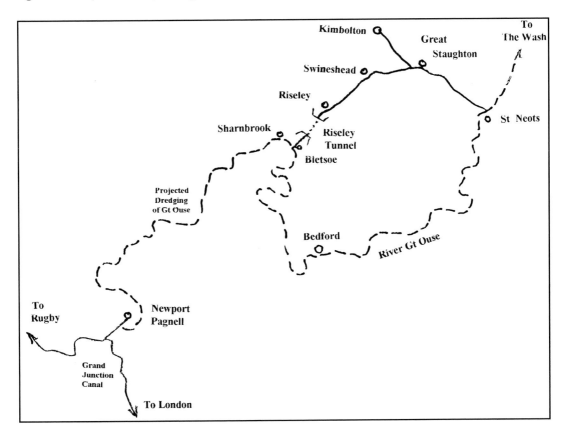

The Millington scheme, as shown in the accompanying map, was for twenty-ton narrow-boats and was designed to link the Grand Junction Canal from the terminus of the mile-long Newport Pagnell Canal branch with St. Neots, fourteen miles downstream of Bedford on the Great Ouse. It was proposed that the canal would use a partially dredged River Great Ouse from Newport Pagnell downstream to Sharnbrook, six miles north of Bedford.

The route would then become totally canalised, leaving the main river at Bletsoe to strike north-eastwards in a cutting towards North End Farm by means of a flight of locks, only to be forced into an impressive two and three-quarter mile-long tunnel under Riseley Hill and the western edge of the present-day Thurleigh Airfield.

It was calculated that the cost of this tunnel would be about £27,000, so Millington added a proposal for an alternative shorter half-mile tunnel scheme burrowing into the hill higher up. Extra locks and a steam engine for pumping Great Ouse water to the higher level were included in the second idea in an attempt to reduce costs and thus make the scheme more attractive to potential investors. There would be no building access problems over this canal section for it was through and under his Lordship's Bletsoe land.

The tunnel was designed to emerge into daylight on the edge of Riseley village and the canal would follow the stream, Riseley Brook, and the turnpike road to Swineshead, where it would swing eastwards through a broad natural gravel-based valley to Pertenhall and Great Staughton, "swinging close to Mr Banks's Tile Kiln" in the latter place. From there, the canal would continue on its route to Hail Weston and St. Neots through a few locks and cuttings, finally to emerge into the main river one hundred yards upstream of the confluence of the Great Ouse and Kym rivers. The Little Paxton Paper Mill, a few hundred yards downstream from this confluence, was mentioned in the survey so as to enhance the commercial viability of the venture to any potential subscriber (the paper mill is still in existence today). The canal's final two furlongs would have bisected the present-day St. Neots golf course by means of a cutting.

John Millington attempted to make the scheme more attractive by proposing the construction of a three mile branch from Great Staughton back upstream in the River Kym valley to serve Kimbolton, the terminus being on the Stonely side of the town. For whatever reason, maybe the cost of the tunnel and aqueducts being influential, this whole canal scheme failed to materialise, and Kimbolton slumbered on for a few more decades.

Fig 2 - Traffic on the River Great Ouse Approaching St Neots from Upstream in 1818

The Early Growth of Railways

Before examining Kimbolton's small, but important, role in railway history, we must first examine briefly the wider railway scene.

The earliest lines, such as the Stockton & Darlington Railway of 1825, were built with the aim of exploiting the country's mineral resources. The additional idea of the mass transport of passengers emanated from the opening of the Liverpool & Manchester Railway in 1830, and this led to hundreds of independent schemes being proposed, many of which were ill-conceived. This brought about the 'railway-mania' years of the mid-1840's when a large number of schemes failed due to a lack of adequate finance.

The final nail in the coffin for this first period of railway building was precipitated in February 1849 by the exposure of the York-based 'railway king' George Hudson and his illegal share dealings, by Mr Robert Prance of the London Stock Exchange, at the half-yearly meeting of the York, Newcastle & Berwick Railway Company.

The resultant enquiries opened many cans of worms over artificially inflated railway share values and manipulated dividends involving companies all around the north of England. The immediate loss of faith brought a dramatic drop in railway construction. Money supply suddenly dried up and people were reluctant to invest in shares for new schemes. Mortgages to finance railway schemes were difficult to negotiate with the banks. All this brought about some semblance of order to the national scene and there then followed a more sensible and legal approach in the early 1850's.

The Railway that was Never Built

In the early 1840's no railway line existed in the Bedford-Sandy-Huntingdon-Kettering area, the nearest being at Bletchley and owned by the London & Birmingham Railway. Our story starts when a railway line was projected and surveyed from just south of Leicester to Kettering, Bedford and Hitchin with a branch line from Kettering, through Raunds and Bythorn and down the valley to Huntingdon along the present-day route of the A1-M1 Road Link, more commonly known as the A14 Trunk Road. The railway was planned during the 'mania' years in the form of the Midland Railway's "Extension to Hitchin, Northampton and Huntingdon Railway Act, 1847" (which was surveyed in 1845).

The 1847 Act of Parliament gave the Midland Railway permission to build a branch line to diverge from the main Leicester-Bedford-Hitchin proposed main line at Isham, just south of Kettering, and head for Huntingdon along the line *"through, or into several parishes, townships, and places of Isham, Burton Latimer, Finedon (otherwise Thingdon), Great Addington, Little Addington, and Raunds in the county of Northampton; Keyston, Bythorn, Molesworth, Great Catworth, Leighton Bromeswold, Spaldwick, Ellington, Easton, Alconbury, Little Stukely, Great Stukely, St John Huntingdon, St Mary Huntingdon, Brampton, and Godmanchester in the county of Huntingdon, and terminating at or near the town of Huntingdon in the parish of Godmanchester by a junction with the line of the Ely and Huntingdon Railway Company (eventually to become Huntingdon East Station) ...."*.

The plans also included a proposal for "a branch from the Huntingdon Line to join the Northampton & Peterborough Railway in Irthlingborough: to be built from Raunds Parish through Stanwick to Irthlingborough (Northants.)". This small branch line was never built.

The main line from Raunds down the A14 trunk road route, if it had been built, would have used the valley of the river, which is locally known as 'The Brook', from Bythorn, two miles east of Thrapston, eastwards to the present A14-A1 junction at Brampton Hut and on into Godmanchester. The valley is a shallow wide trough through glaciated lowland with a skim of outwash gravels and sands along its base, thus providing good drainage for a railway track-bed, and would have been attractive to potential engineers and surveyors alike.

The route was surveyed by JG Binns in conjunction with two engineers, namely Robert Stephenson and Charles Liddell. Robert Stephenson's career eventually became so high profile it was the nation's wish to bury him in Westminster Abbey when he died.

The plans were deposited with the appropriate authority in London for consideration on November 30th 1845. These men were 'railway giants' in the eyes of the nation at the time and it was no surprise when the plans were given the Royal Assent in 1847.

The Midland Railway Company was in its infancy at this time and had been skilfully sculpted a mere three years earlier, in 1844, by 'King' George Hudson with the amalgamation of the North Midland, Midland Counties (of Thomas Cook Fame) and Birmingham & Derby Junction Companies and was based in Derby.

Like Father, Like Son

The geographical character of the valley of 'The Brook' is probably what attracted the original engineer, Robert Stephenson, son of the famous railway pioneer, George, and JG Binns to that route. A detailed study of the 1845 plans, ideally exemplified and illustrated in Figure 1 from Spaldwick Parish, highlights a number of interesting features that will be discussed shortly.

The submitted survey shows that the proposed route was not restricted to a narrow path. The surveyor was allowed a certain amount of deviation to provide for any unexpected problems, such as drainage and geology, once construction had begun. The actual route tended to be sited mostly on the valley bottom land, a few metres north of 'The Brook'. Occasionally, the route would find itself on the south side, but all the time keeping to the gentlest gradients and the cheapest land. The plans did not include bridges or brook realignments of meanders to ease engineering problems, but these details would have been incorporated later after the Act had been passed.

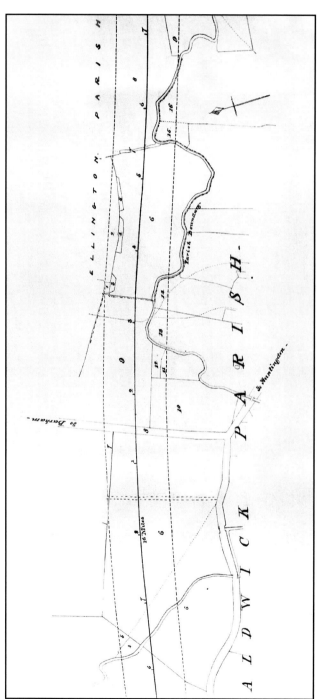

Fig 3 - Projected 1845 Route of Railway through Spaldwick & Ellington Parishes eight miles west of Huntingdon

It is worth comparing the style of these plans with a set of available plans drawn by George Stephenson in 1837 when he was constructing the North Midland Railway between Chesterfield and Clay Cross, four miles to the south. The route runs along the valley of the north-flowing River Rother which contains very similar physical geographical features found along the valley containing the current A14 trunk road to the west of Huntingdon.

Both sets of plans (1837 and 1845) show routes that follow the land nearest to the river in both cases. It might be that the father's skills may well have been handed down to his son (and the latter was willing to listen to the former!). In addition, Robert's surveyor on the 1845 route, JG Binns, was probably closely related to George's personal secretary, Charles Binns. Maybe one of their professional strengths emanated from this continuity of teamwork and build-up of experience.

The illustration below has been added to show how the 1845 route would have linked into the proposed Ely & Huntingdon Railway at Godmanchester. This route would have been an ideal east-west link between the Midlands and Cambridge, but it was never built.

Above: Fig 4 - Robert Stephenson

Below: Fig 5 - George Stephenson's 1837 North Midland Railway Map one Mile South of Chesterfield

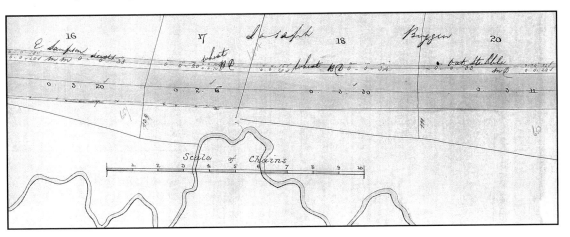

The 1847 Act was not implemented immediately. The cost of building was going to be a staggering £2,250,000 and raising that sort of finance would take time. However, when the plans re-emerged a few years later, the competition for building railways to London from the North Midlands was very fierce. Much behind-the-scenes wheeler-dealing occurred between the companies and landowners to the point where branch lines were bartered and discarded by the negotiators so as to allow the major jig-saw of main lines to evolve into the pattern that became familiar in the second half of the Nineteenth Century.

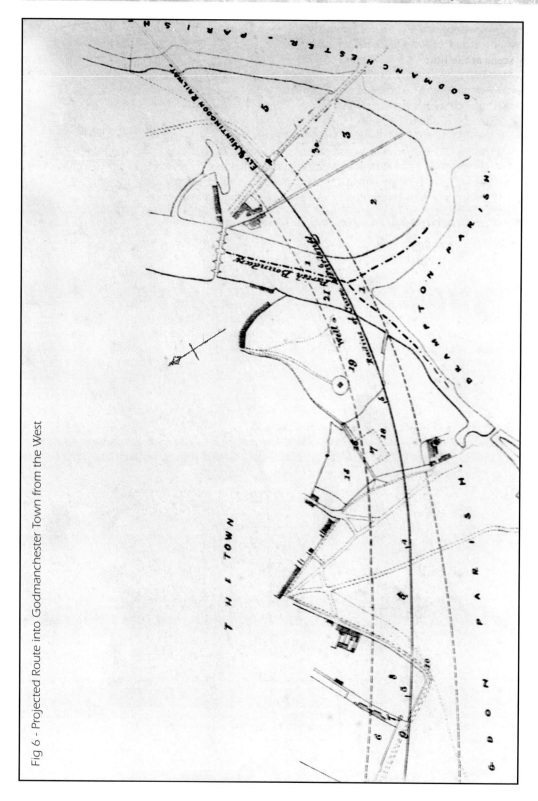

Fig 6 - Projected Route into Godmanchester Town from the West

It was in this way that the Kettering to Huntingdon branch line, approved in the 1847 Act, fell by the wayside and ended up in the 'dustbin' of unbuilt railway line proposals that littered the railway scene at the time.

Occasionally, cartographers in the mid-Nineteenth Century were caught out by these ephemeral schemes as exemplified by Sidney Hall's 1850 map extract of Huntingdonshire, located on pages 10 & 11. The map shows the Kettering to Huntingdon Railway on the proposed 1845 route thus rendering this map obsolete within a short space of time.

I wonder how important this route would have been today with the evolution of the European Union and the need for an east-west railway route, to deal with the Felixstowe container traffic, growing evermore urgent. Doubtless, the British penchant for the ostrich-like head burying music hall act by the powers that be will come into play, see any plans for such a route dashed and condemn life along the A14 Trunk Road Corridor to a further slice of misery.

The Local Kimbolton Scene from 1850

The second stage of major railway building, in the middle of the Nineteenth Century, was dominated by the overwhelming attraction of London. The magnetism of the capital - at the time probably the most influential city in the world - acted as a hub from which the major lines radiated like the spokes of a wheel. The Great Northern Railway, for example, was opened through St. Neots in 1850 (Act of Parliament - 1845) on its way north to Doncaster to link up with the already well-established network of that area.

The Midland Railway finally extended its main line southwards from Leicester to Bedford, and on to Cardington, Shefford and Hitchin, on May 8th 1857. This was part of the abandoned proposal of 1847, which had been re-constituted under the Midland Railway (Leicester and Hitchin) Act of 1853. One major omission from this new scheme, however, was the Kettering to Huntingdon branch line.

When the Bedford to Hitchin line opened, an agreement allowed Midland Railway trains to use the Great Northern Railway Company's lines from Hitchin southwards and also its facilities at King's Cross. While this provided the Midland with an alternative route to the capital from that via Rugby and the London & North Western Railway, transits were soon found to be more expensive and often subject to delay, as the Great Northern naturally gave preference to its own traffic on what soon became a very congested stretch of line.

Fig 7 - St Pancras Passenger Station in the late Nine-teenth Century

In fact, the congestion caused by this dual company use of the Great Northern line had been anticipated from the outset when the 1847 Act of Parliament was passed, and Section 61 stated that "the Midland Railway Company shall pay to the Great Northern Railway Company the sum of fifty pounds per hour, by way of penalty, for every hour during which such interruption shall continue ...."

Matters came to a head on June 30th 1862 when the Great Northern Railway was forced to ban Midland trains from entering King's Cross until the situation had cleared. Shortly afterwards, the Midland decided to build its own direct line from Bedford, via Luton, to London St Pancras, which was then known as Agar Town. The station canopy, the largest single-span structure in the world at the time and built by the Butterley Iron & Engineering Company of Ripley, Derbyshire, did not open until October 1868. Kimbolton did actually receive goods traffic from St Pancras early in 1866, however, but this was via the branch from the Great Northern Railway, which was opened for mineral (coal) traffic in 1862 and goods traffic in 1865.

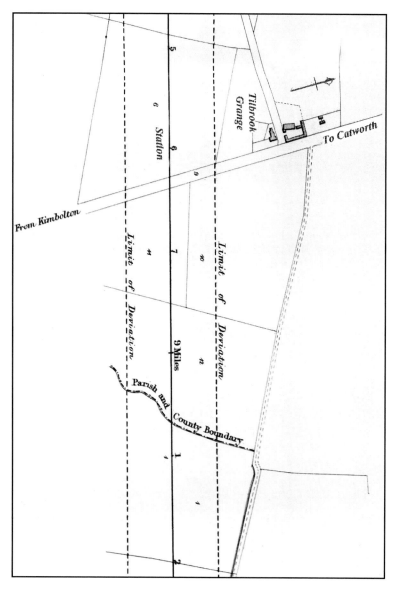

This historical precis suggests that, from 1850, when the railway arrived in St Neots, any Kimbolton-bound goods from London were originally sent from King's Cross via St Neots Station and then by road for the last eight miles. After February 21st 1866, when Kimbolton Station opened, goods traffic would have been routed from St Pancras via Hitchin, Bedford and Kettering. Passengers would have travelled by the same routes, using King's Cross until October 1868 when St Pancras opened for passenger traffic.

The history of these major routes is, hopefully, a help in understanding Kimbolton's place in the regional network jigsaw.

Fig 8 - Plan of the 1863 Kimbolton Station Site adjacent to the Catworth Turnpike Road and Survey Details of the Proposed Station Road Bridge

The Kettering, Thrapston and Huntingdon Railway

The aborted proposal for a line running east from Kettering, contained in the Midland Railway's Act of 1847, was resurrected in 1862, but on a different route, by the passing of the Kettering & Thrapstone Railway Act, one of the prime objectives being to exploit the newly-opened iron ore deposits around the Thrapston area. Thrapston was not on the original 1845 route, but now there was the attraction of lucrative mineral traffic. The line was to terminate adjacent to the London & North Western Railway's Northampton to Peterborough line on the western edge of the town.

A further Act was passed the following year, which extended the line forward, this time 'along the tops', through Kimbolton and Grafham, to Huntingdon (see locational fig. 41). This idea, to move the proposed 1845 line two miles to the south of the original route, was put forward in 1862. The Act, called the Kettering, Thrapstone & Huntingdon Railway Act, was given the Royal Assent in the following year. The plan looped south-eastwards from Thrapston to Raunds and on to Kimbolton.

The land to be purchased for the construction of the line belonged mostly to the Duke of Manchester, who had increased his land ownership by marrying, in 1822, the heiress Millicent Sparrow of Brampton Park, which was located in the western approaches to Huntingdon. She owned extensive tracts of agricultural land between Grafham and Huntingdon. This meant that a land sale deal could be struck almost totally between the company and the Duke if he was approached in the right manner. The discreet, political approach is brilliantly described in the booklet "The Kettering-Huntingdon Line" by John Rhodes, which is full of wonderful information and local anecdotes. The Duke willingly allowed the sale of land to go forward.

High values were given to the land along the proposed route, which varied from £60 on average up to £300 an acre (see Appendix 5 for imperial to metric conversions) in the Buckden area where the land was of greater agricultural value. An inflation chart converts these figures into very comfortable present-day values of £3,000 and £15,000 respectively. Doubtless, the Duke would have been very grateful to his estate agent for negotiating such a good deal with the railway company. Local knowledge indicates that the Duke of Manchester refused to allow the line to be built any nearer to Kimbolton than it was, and he made sure the railway was kept out of sight and over the horizon two miles to the north of Kimbolton.

Fig 9 - Kettering, Thrapston & Huntingdon Railway Company Share Certificate reproduced directly from the original copper printing plate

The company changed its name to the Kettering, Thrapston & Huntingdon Railway on July 23rd 1863 (the name 'Thrapstone' officially lost its 'e' on October 1st 1885), and was not absorbed fully into the Midland Railway until 1897. Two engineers were appointed for the planning of the route, namely George C Bruce and James Brunlees.

James Brunlees, Engineer in charge of the Railway's Construction

James Brunlees was an exceptional gentleman and came with a most prestigious engineering reputation. He was born at Kelso south of Edinburgh on January 5th 1816. It was only through sheer deter-mination to better himself, coupled with considerable intelligence, that led him into railway construction. After leaving school his father put him into gardening and farm work with the intention of becoming a landscape gardener, but James was keen to pursue a more academic career. He saved enough money from his early jobs to pay for two study sessions at Edinburgh University. His potential was identified by Alexander Adie, by whom he was engaged in 1838 as his assistant on the building of the Bolton & Preston Railway.

Later, he joined the staff of Locke and Errington, and played an important part in the laying of the railway line from Beattock to Carstairs, with branches to Glasgow and Edinburgh. This layout forms the basis of the northernmost section of today's West Coast Main Line north of Carlisle.

Fig 10 - Sir James Brunlees - President of the Institute of Civil Engineers

By the time Brunlees acquired the Kettering to Huntingdon Railway job he had carved out an illustrious career in railway construction. On completion of the Beattock line he was appointed as acting engineer under Sir John Hawkshaw, engineer-in-chief to the Lancashire & Yorkshire Railway. At the age of 34 years Brunlees went to Ireland to take charge of the construction of the Londonderry & Coleraine Railway. Two years later he undertook the difficult task of building the Ulverston & Lancaster Railway, which demanded inventing a new method of digging down through 20 metres of treacherous soft sand to reach solid rock, on the northern edge of Morcambe Bay.

Subsequently Brunlees took a leading role in engineering work of all kinds in addition to acting as arbitrator in the settlement of disputed contracts, and other railway matters, both at home and abroad. Other major schemes he carried out included the one and a quarter mile-long Solway Firth Viaduct, the Clifton Extension Railway, the Avonmouth, King's Lynn, and Whitehaven docks, and the piers at the rapidly growing seaside resorts of Southport, Southend, New Brighton and Llandudno.

Abroad, Brunlees was in great demand for his expertise. He was responsible for the Mont Cenis Summit Railway, involving very steep gradients, the Santos & Sao Paulo Railway in Brazil with its cable-worked inclines, the Central Uruguay and other railways in South America and elsewhere. After Sao Paulo, he came direct to the Kettering to Huntingdon Railway job!

Brunlees also became joint senior engineer for the attempt at constructing the first Channel Tunnel in 1872, the entrance to which can still be seen at the base of the cliff near Folkestone. This venture was soon aborted and the boring machines remained abandoned in place until the present Channel Tunnel scheme began in the 1980's. The other joint senior engineer on the 1872 project was Sir John Hawkshaw, his old boss from the Lancashire & Yorkshire Railway days.

In 1881 Brunlees went on to build, jointly, with another great railway engineer, Sir Charles Fox, the Mersey Tunnel Railway under that famous estuary from Liverpool to Birkenhead. All these engineering achievements brought him to the attention of the Government and he was was knighted in May 1886 by Queen Victoria. He became President of the Institute of Civil Engineers and a Fellow of the Royal Society of Edinburgh. His death occurred on June 2nd 1892 in Wimbledon at the age of seventy six.

Brunlees was buried in Brookwood Cemetery near Woking, Surrey. His body was probably transported by the unique Brookwood Necropolis Railway, which operated this unusual service from a private station near Victoria Station, down the London & South Western Railway, to one of two railway stations specially built within the huge cemetery. This rail service ceased after the London depot was bombed in 1941. The Brookwood Cemetery Society today tends Sir James Brunlees grave with the help of his great great grandson, James, the last surviving person in the United Kingdom with the surname (apart from the latter's two sons!).

The cemetery contains a number of famous remains. The latest was Dodi Fayed, whose body was temporarily stored in the first ever United Kingdom's Muslim section before removal to its permanent resting place elsewhere.

Fig 11 - Sir James Brunlees Grave in Brookwood Cemetery

Further Planning and Running Details

At the eastern end of the line, the 1845 proposal to run directly into the Ely & Huntingdon Railway was retained this time by means of a sharp curve. The new route brought the line into contact with the Great Northern just north of Buckden, and thus ran parallel to the main line for one mile northwards to Huntingdon. The idea of a short branch line was added to this 1862 plan which linked the Midland Railway to the Great Northern at Huntingdon North Station.

Fig 12 - Proposed Junction at Huntingdon in the 1863 Plans

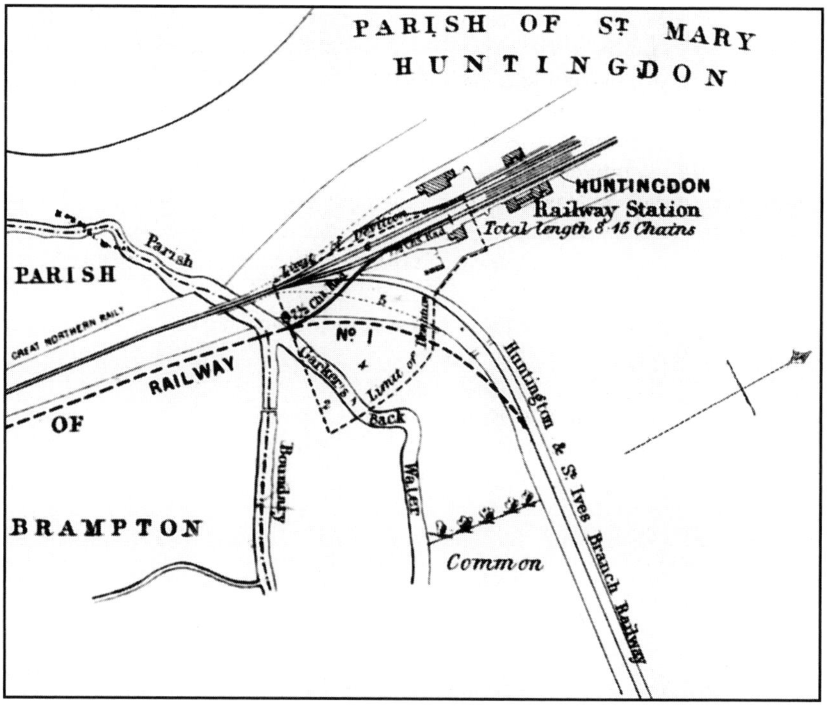

The line was duly constructed, and subsequently opened throughout for goods on February 21st and for passengers on March 1st 1866. Although built by a nominally independent company, this project was very much under the auspices of the Midland Railway, which worked the line from the onset. The Midland was granted running powers over the Ely & Huntingdon line to St Ives, and onwards over the Great Eastern Railway's own line from St Ives to Cambridge. Here the Midland built a motive power depot, and opened a booking office at the station. This provided the Midland Railway with the opportunity to run through trains from Kettering all the way to Cambridge, though restrictions were placed on passengers between St Ives and Cambridge. These are explained beneath the following 'Weekdays Only' timetable.

WEEK-DAYS. NOVEMBER, 1869

Miles from Cambridge			1 2 GOV	1 2 Class	1 2 GOV	1 2 Class
..	† CAMBRIDGE ..	dep.	7 15	11 35	2 26	6 5
4¾	† Histon	,,	7 25	.....	2 30	6 15
6¾	† Oakington ..	,,	7 29	..	2 35	6 20
9¾	† Long Stanton ..	,,	7 35	.....	2 42	6 26
11¾	† Swavesey	,,	7 41	..	2 47	6 32
14¾	† St. Ives..........	,,	7 49	12 4	2 55	6 46
19½	† HUNTINGDON	,,	8 0	12 16	3 5	6 50
23	Buckden		8 8	G	3 13	6 53
25¾	Graffham		8 16	.. | ..	3 21	7 6
30¾	Kimbolton		8 29	12 37	3 34	7 19
35¾	Raunds		8 40	F	3 45	7 30
38¾	THRAPSTONE		8 49	12 52	3 54	7 39
40¾	Twywell		8 56	..	4 1	7 46
43	Cranford		9 3	.....	4 8	7 53
47¾	KETTERING ..	arr.	9 15	1 10	4 20	8 5

		1 2 GOV	1 2 Class	1 2 Class	1 2 GOV
KETTERING ...	dep.	7 38	11 6	2 50	7 10
Cranford	..	7 50	11 17	.. | ..	7 22
Twywell		7 57	C	.....	7 29
THRAPSTONE	..	8 7	11 27	3 10	7 39
Raunds		8 17	11 37	3 19	7 49
Kimbolton ..	..	8 29	11 48	3 33	8 1
Graffham		8 41	11 59	.....	8 13
Buckden ..	..	8 47	12 5	..	8 19
* HUNTINGDON	arr.	8 55	12 15	3 53	8 27
* St. Ives ..	,,	9 6	12 26	4 3	8 37
* Swavesey	,,	9 13	12 32	.....	8 44
* Long Stanton	,,	9 18	12 38	..	8 49
* Oakington	,,	9 21	12 45	.....	8 54
* Histon ..	,,	9 29	12 49	4 23	8 59
* CAMBRIDGE .	,,	9 43	1 0	4 35	9 10

Fig 13 - Timetable for 1869 Kettering to Cambridge

! - Trains from Cambridge to Kettering marked to Stop at Histon, Oakington Long Stanton, Swavesey, St Ives and Huntingdon only stop when required to take up Passengers booked to Stations West of Huntingdon. Passengers are not booked between Cambridge and Huntingdon, and the Intermediate Stations by Midland Trains.

* - Trains from Kettering to Cambridge marked to stop at Huntingdon, St Ives, Swavesey, Long Stanton, Oakington, and Histon only stop when required to set down Passengers booked from Stations West of Huntingdon. Passengers are not booked between Huntingdon and Cambridge, and the Intermediate Stations by Midland Trains.

A detailed photographic and cartographic record of the whole line is contained in the book "Branch Lines around Huntingdon - Kettering to Cambridge" by Allan Mott and Christopher Awdry (of "Thomas the Tank Engine" fame), which was reprinted in 1999. I am indebted to them for permission to quote material from their publication. Their work supported earlier research by Professor Pat White of Keele University, who retired to Godmanchester after an illustrious academic career in geographical studies.

It is fortunate that a reasonable amount of the original paperwork from the earliest years of Kimbolton Station, on the Kettering-Huntingdon line, still exists. This publication analyses the information in these documents and, it is hoped, will provide you with an interesting insight into the working of a country railway station, and the changes its coming brought to the local community in the middle of the Nineteenth Century.

Fig 14 - View of Kimbolton Station in the 1930's

Here it Comes!

The Kettering to Huntingdon line was officially opened on February 21st 1866 for goods and March 1st for passengers, though it is possible that the 'Special Train' recorded in the station's log book on February 27th conveyed invited guests. The log-book, which was used by the station staff to record every single daily incident from the arrival of the first train on February 21st, has recently been discovered and clearly demonstrates how the newly opened rural station came into operation. The first seven months of trials and tribulations are recorded in the log-book and a cross selection of some of the events can be found in Appendix 1.

The first train brought a cart and a machine from Derby. The first invoice handled by the station was to order a coal shipment from Pinxton, a village on the Derbyshire-Nottinghamshire border, and renowned for its coal quality. Subsequent orders for coal in 1866 nearly all came from collieries within a few miles of Pinxton. They were Nether Birchwood and Coates Park in the village of Somercotes, and Ripley Colliery (see Appendix 2).

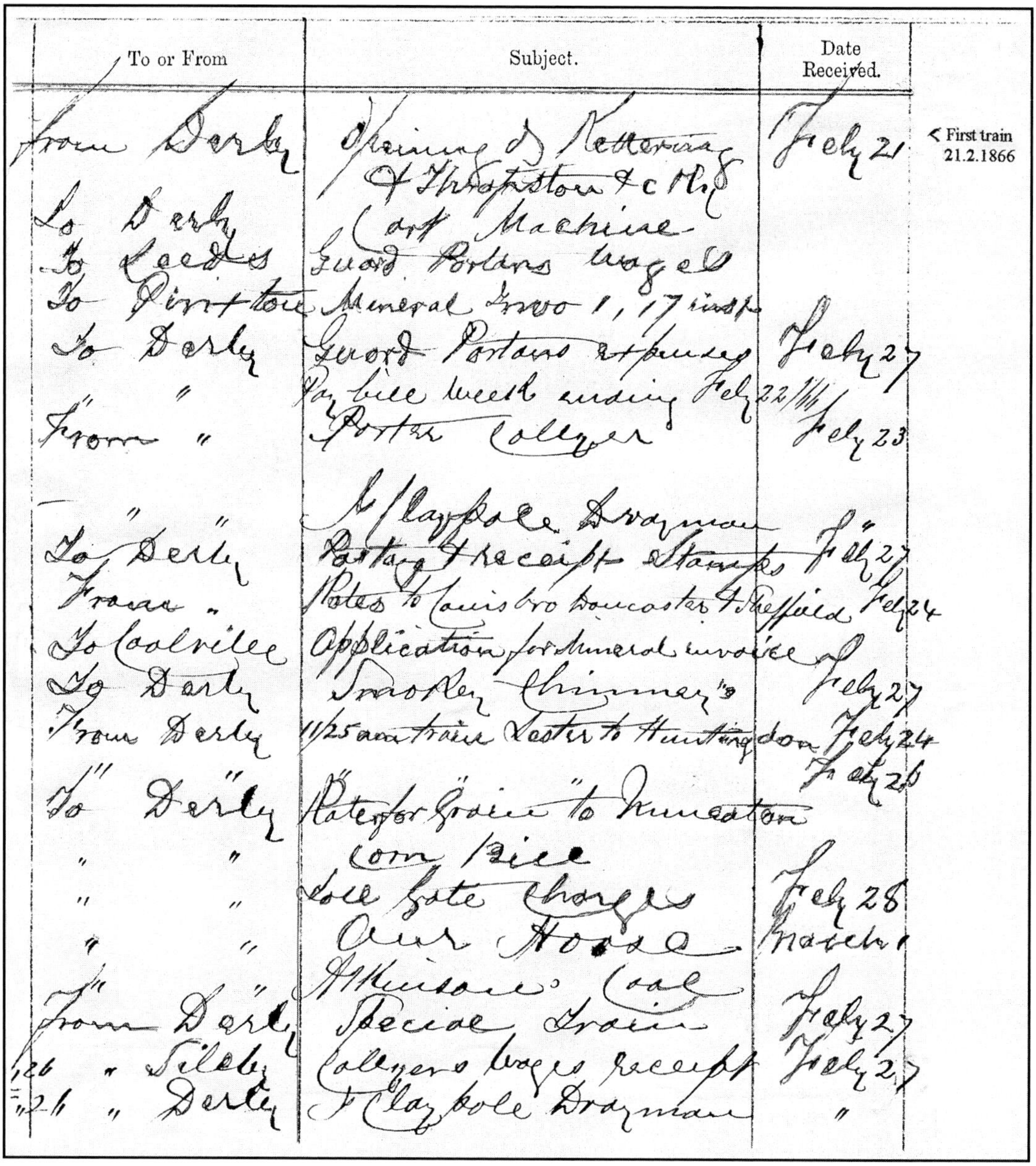

To or From	Subject.	Date Received.
From Derby	Opening of Kettering & Thrapston &c Rly	Feby 21 ‹ First train 21.2.1866
To Derby	Cart Machine	
To Leeds	Guard Porters wages	
To Pinxton	Mineral Invo 1, 17 inst	
To Derby	Guard Porters expenses	Feby 27
" "	Pay bill week ending Feby 22/66	
From "	Porter Collyer	Feby 23
	A Claypole Drayman	
To Derby	Posting & receipt stamps	Feby 27
From "	Rates to Louisbro Doncaster & Sheffield	Feby 24
To Coalville	Application for Mineral invoice	
To Derby	Smokey Chimneys	Feby 27
From Derby	11/25 am train Leester to Huntingdon	Feby 24 / Feby 26
To Derby	Rates for Grain to Nuneaton	
" "	Corn Bill	
" "	Toll Gate Charges	Feby 28
" "	Our House	March 1
" "	Atkinsons Coal	
From Derby	Special Train	Feby 27
26 " Sileby	Collyers wages receipt	Feby 27
21 " Derby	& Claypole Drayman	"

Fig 15 - Opening of Railway : Log of First Week's Working

This revelation came as quite a shock to me because the first two settlements were the origins of my family and school friends, and the coal from Ripley was mined from beneath the very fields in which I passed my very happy, constructive(?) childhood days playing sport and digging practice coal-mine tunnels through the nearby railway embankment. After all, the most likely employment was as a miner when I left school in the middle of the last century!

As staff were engaged at Kimbolton Station their names were entered in the log book. Those whose names appeared in the first week included:-

Fig 16 - Locations of Coal-mines Supplying Kimbolton in 1866

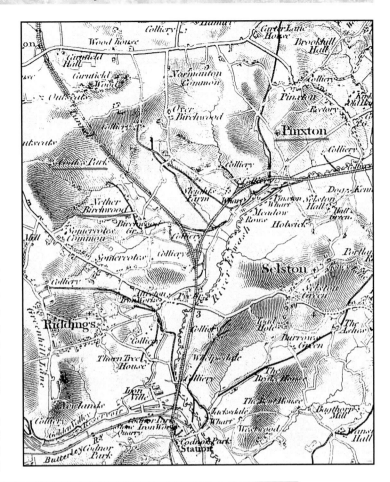

Guard - Mr. Portans; Porters - Messrs. Collyer, Partridge, Flinders and Doffern; Drayman - Mr Claypole.

These men were employed after satisfying the Company over the quality of their academic ability, health and character. Arithmetic and writing quality were strong requirements before a clerk's job was offered to an applicant. Here is an extract from a typical application form for a job with a railway company in that era, even though it was thirty years after the Kettering to Huntingdon line was opened. The applicant in this case was thirteen years old and had just left school at the end of the Nineteenth Century.

Was Kimbolton Station fully equipped for efficient service from day one? Not at all! The office equipment

TERMS and Conditions upon which Station Masters and Clerks are admitted to the Service of the Lancashire, Derbyshire and East Coast Railway.

1.—No application can be considered from anyone who is not prepared to devote his whole time and attention to the business of the Company.

2.—Appointments are made on the distinct understanding that applicants hold themselves in readiness to proceed to duty immediately on being summoned, and that they reside wherever required, pay being allowed from date of employment.

3.—Candidates who have had a previous engagement or engagements must produce testimonials of character from previous employers. Juniors who have not had any previous appointment will be required to produce a testimonial from their Schoolmaster. All candidates will be required to produce a certificate of birth, and testimonials as to character from two respectable householders.

4.—Juniors will be required to pass an examination in writing, arithmetic and other subjects to the satisfaction of the Company.

5.—Candidates who have not had previous Railway experience will be taken on trial for one month, and will not be appointed permanently unless the result of the trial is satisfactory.

6.—Candidates for employment will be required to pass the Company's examination for colour and distance vision, and must also produce a certificate, from a Medical man selected by the Company, that they are free from any bodily complaint and of strong constitution.

Fig 17 - Terms of Railway Employment in 1890

arrived in dribs and drabs during the next fortnight. The station was sent a log-book in which to record all railway and station business, however minor, but it was replaced by a range of more specialized books and paperwork at the end of November in the first year of operation.

Two goods trains visited the station on February 24th and 26th. On each occasion the train arrived at 11.25am from Leicester. Then the first train to be designated a "Special" arrived from Derby on February 27th 1866. Although it has been stated previously that Kimbolton Station officially opened for passengers on March 1st, there is no mention of such a train arriving in the log book and, considering the more petty nature of many other entries, I am surprised by this omission. This may confirm the theory on the previous page that this special train conveyed passengers - albeit not fare-paying ones. The first Midland Railway passenger timetable for this line was issued for March 1866 and extracts can be found in Appendix Four.

At that time of year it was cold enough to need a coal fire in the station and this resulted in a message being sent to Derby stating that the chimneys were "smokey". This first full week of operation saw the first business with St. Pancras Station. An agent wished to send a load of barley to London and a rate for the job was requested from the Derby headquarters of the Midland Railway Company. In addition, a jubilant Mr. Collyer received his first wages from the company's Leicester office.

Kimbolton Station's offices were gradually stocked with missing equipment. On the first full day, postage and receipt stamps were requested from Derby (railway companies issued their own stamps). Passenger fares' tables arrived just in time for the first passengers, while on March 1st a figure no. 6 was delivered for the ticket dating machine! Further requests were telegraphed to Derby for a ticket punch, paper files and timetables. An order was also sent for whiting (for platform and step edge highlighting) and dusters. A cash box arrived from Leicester. The first horse to be handled by the station was loaded for Derby. It is not known what the staff used for seats in the station office because three desks and stools were not requested until March 28th!

Celebrations all round! It was obvious Kimbolton people rolled out the barrel for the opening of the railway. The first ale to arrive by rail in the locality came from one of the best brewing centres, namely Burton-on-Trent, on March 2nd. On the following day, a telegraph post was causing an obstruction, hopefully not through staff inebriation, so had to be removed. On the same day the first load of granite paving setts arrived from Mountsorrel, Leicestershire.

On the 4th of March a significant order was telegraphed from the station and was the first order to be sent out by rail for Mr T Smith and was for barley to Peterborough. This was the first reference to the Smith family, and their position in the local commercial structure will be explored in detail later. The Smith family members had the chance to be well-educated for, although they originated from Great Catworth, they could have attended the school in the adjacent village of Tilbrook to provide them with the skills to enter commercial life.

On the same day as Mr Smith's first order a goods train steamed through the station from Leicester to Huntingdon at 11.25 am. March 7th saw the first farm animals despatched for market by train.

They were poultry (plus eggs) and were destined for St Pancras. On the next day pigs were loaded for Birmingham, and another horse left for Derby.

On March 7th, a notice of "Toll Gate Charges" was received from Derby, which may well have related to the turnpike (toll) road that passed by the station from Kimbolton to Catworth.

During the first five months of goods handling, coal deliveries show an interesting pattern. The opening of the railway saw a flurry of activity with Mr. Kinson, a local man, leading the way with registered orders which were mainly from the Pinxton area, although one each came from Coalville and Mexborough. In the first month of the station's existence ten orders arrived, but deliveries petered out rapidly after March. Was the cost too great? Was the local timber supply too good for this new fuel to compete effectively or was the summer arriving? More will be mentioned about coal supplies later.

One local coal merchant did try to take advantage of the opening of the Kettering to Huntingdon Railway. Clark & Company, coal merchants, were already based at the Great Northern Railway Station at Huntingdon, and an advertisement was placed in the St Neots Chronicle newspaper to announce that the company had commenced to sell coal at Kimbolton, Grafham and Brampton Stations, and Stow Siding. This was at the end of February 1866.

Fig 18 - Establishment of Coal Selling at Stations along the Line

> ## HUNTINGDON AND KETTERING RAILWAY,
> ## COALS ! COALS ! COALS !
>
> MESSRS. CLARK & CO., Coal Merchants, Great Northern Railway Station, Huntingdon, beg to inform the Public that they have commenced to Sell the following description of Coals at the Kimbolton, Stow, Graffham, and Brampton Stations of this Railway, at the lowest possible prices for CASH, namely :—
>
> Best Derby Hards, Ditto Softs, Silkstones, Staveley, and other House Coals.
>
> N.B.— Orders sent to any of the above-mentioned Stations immediately attended to.—Contracts made for any period of time.

A Further Stephenson Family Connection

There is one, but it is very tenuous! If you study the deliveries' list for the station in the first seven months of operation (Appendix 1), there are two references to lime arriving from the Clay Cross Company. The orders came from Clay Cross and Ambergate, both in central East Derbyshire. This lime was for either agricultural and/or gas-purifying (see later) purposes, and was advertised by the company as "the best quality in the country". Any farmers, industrialists and geologists who read this book may find the following data interesting;

Analysis of Ambergate (Crich) Lime from Clay Cross Co. Records 1930

Lime Analysis Per Cent

Lime (CaO)	*96.28*
Magnesia (MgO)	*0.36*
Silica (SiO2)	*1.44*
Oxides of Iron & Manganese	*0.25*
Sulphuric Acid (SO3)	*0.27*
Phosphorus & Arsenic	*absent*
Combined H2O & Carbonic Acid	*1.40*
	100.0

The company was set up by the great man himself in 1837, as "Geo. Stephenson & Co." the name changing to "Clay Cross & Co." in 1852, four years after his death in 1848 and the disposal of the Stephenson family's shares by Robert. The company grew thereafter in strength through iron smelting, coal mining and engineering until the 1960's when gradual departmental economic down-turns led to a final total extinction of the company as recently as 2000.

During the construction of the North Midland Railway between Leeds and Derby, in the period from 1836 to 1840, George Stephenson discovered coking coal and iron ore within the Clay Cross Tunnel during its excavation. The third raw material required in iron production in a blast furnace is limestone and this was discovered nearby at Crich with additional resources at Ashover being exploited later.

Stephenson decided to exploit these resources and make an even greater fortune. His main lime kilns, were on the North Midland Railway at Ambergate, six miles south of Matlock. They produced 'Crich Lime' and used limestone from Crich Quarry, one mile to the north, now famous as the site of the National Tram Museum. The following photograph of the lime kilns shows the self-acting rope railway incline in the background down which the limestone travelled from the quarry until its closure in the early 1950's. This was how the Kimbolton-bound lime started its journey.

Another Stephenson connection with the line concerned George's son Robert. His Darlington steam engine company built five of the 480 Class locomotives which are recorded as having worked through Kimbolton in 1869 (see Appendix 4).

Fig 19 - Ambergate Limeworks, Derbyshire

PART TWO
The Station Serves the Area

Delivering the Goods

Among the paperwork that has survived from Kimbolton Station are Goods Delivery books. An analysis of the 'Goods Delivery' book for 1868 provides the reader with a wonderful window into daily life in Kimbolton and the surrounding districts at that time. Other 'Goods Delivery' books, for 1871 and 1879-82 enable us to make comparisons and see how trade developed after the station opened.

Another year studied in detail, 1880, provides us with an insight into the character of the outflow of local farm animals to markets beyond the immediate area. Although cities like London were acquiring their fuel from coalfields in the north, their food was being bought from rural auctions, in turn supplied by communities like Kimbolton's rural district.

A brief analysis of the 'Goods Delivery' book for 1868 indicates that its contents are markedly different from the later 1871 book. In 1868 materials arriving were of a more domestic nature and just appeared to serve the shops in Kimbolton and the surrounding villages. Three years later we find local industry was very much to the fore in its usage of the station, the inflow of goods being mainly for wholesalers.

In 1868 food traders were important users of the station's facilities. Mr Giddings, of Kimbolton, seems to have been a grocer, as was Mr Baines. A quick analysis of this book shows there were many direct deliveries of hops. They were usually ordered by Mr Hatfield and came up the Midland Railway from St Pancras. Mr Copland bought a fair amount of beer from Ind Coope in Burton-on-Trent. Mustard arrived in barrels from Cambridge (probably originating from Norwich, still the country's mustard-growing centre), and hundredweight barrels of pepper also helped to activate the local nostrils.

Mr Noble, of Kimbolton, splashed out on a cast-iron bath from Bilston, Staffordshire, while the Duke of Manchester rejoiced with a case of music. Cheese orders arrived from Leicester on many occasions, the north of that county today still being the home of Stilton cheese-making. 'Ice' appears a few times, but so does 'ice sugar', so it is presumed the former is not the frozen variety! The extensive variety of delivered domestic goods received at the station, disappeared from the records by late 1870, and may have been transported in the 'hampers' which appeared in the 1871 'Goods Delivery' book on virtually every page. A list of the most common goods which arrived in 1868 is listed :-

starch   1cwt cask of sugar   2cwt candles tea (London)   vinegar
lead (sheets)   beer (buyer-Hatfield)   gin   mustard ice sugar
lard   bacon   glue   cheese   coffee
fruit hops (buyer-Hatfield)   rice   butter   tobacco
biscuits   copper sheets (Brum)   molasses   calico   slates
malt   box of china (Melton)   carrots   shot   black
oil   cement (St Pancras)   syrup   paper   card
plants   sheep   ointment   bedstead   sago   sulphate
cocoa   saddlery & bridles   shoes   hats   saltpetre

Goods in this year came from a wide range of centres and included:-
Sheffield Thornhill Ardwick Desborough 'City Station'
Bromsgrove Walsall Chesterfield Warrington Bradford
Cradley Chester Worcester Coventry West Bromwich
St Pancras was a major handler of these goods, but orders from this station to Kimbolton had plummeted two years later.

1870-71 Goods Delivery

The 1870-71 'Goods Delivery' book for Kimbolton Station, with its beautiful copper-plate writing, at first glance, appears to be a boring recitation of the station's daily activities, but when each specific

Fig 20 - Extract from 1871 Goods Delivery Book

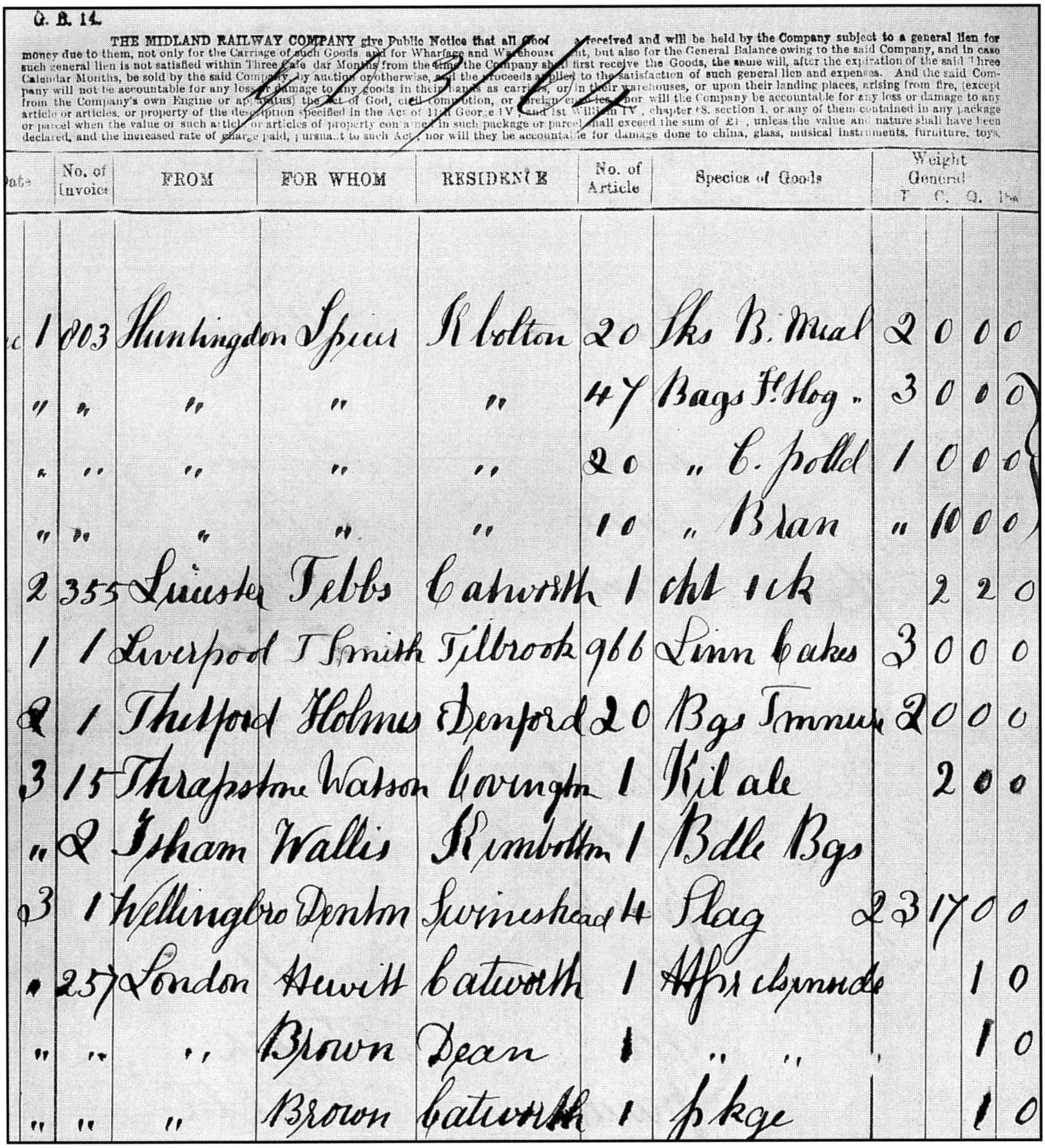

G. B. 14.

THE MIDLAND RAILWAY COMPANY give Public Notice that all Goods are received and will be held by the Company subject to a general lien for money due to them, not only for the Carriage of such Goods and for Wharfage and Warehouse rent, but also for the General Balance owing to the said Company, and in case such general lien is not satisfied within Three Calendar Months from the time the Company shall first receive the Goods, the same will, after the expiration of the said Three Calendar Months, be sold by the said Company, by auction or otherwise, and the proceeds applied to the satisfaction of such general lien and expenses. And the said Company will not be accountable for any loss or damage to any goods in their hands as carriers, or in their warehouses, or upon their landing places, arising from fire, (except from the Company's own Engine or apparatus) the Act of God, civil commotion, or foreign enemies, nor will the Company be accountable for any loss or damage to any article or articles, or property of the description specified in the Act of 11th George IV, and 1st William IV, chapter 68, section 1, or any of them contained in any package or parcel when the value of such article or articles of property contained in such package or parcel shall exceed the sum of £10, unless the value and nature shall have been declared, and the increased rate of charge paid, pursuant to such Act, nor will they be accountable for damage done to china, glass, musical instruments, furniture, toys,

Date	No. of Invoice	FROM	FOR WHOM	RESIDENCE	No. of Article	Species of Goods	Weight General T.	C.	Q.	lbs
1	803	Huntingdon	Spicer	K'bolton	20	Sks B. Meal	2	0	0	0
"	"	"	"	"	47	Bags Fl. Hog.	3	0	0	0
"	"	"	"	"	20	" C. polled	1	0	0	0
"	"	"	"	"	10	" Bran	"	10	0	0
2	355	Leicester	Tebbs	Catworth	1	cht ick		2	2	0
1	1	Liverpool	T Smith	Tilbrook	966	Linn Cakes	3	0	0	0
2	1	Thetford	Holmes	Denford	20	Bgs Manure	2	0	0	0
3	15	Thrapstone	Watson	Covington	1	Kil ale		2	0	0
"	2	Isham	Wallis	Kimbolton	1	Bdle Bgs				
3	1	Wellingbro	Denton	Swineshead	4	Slag	23	17	0	0
"	257	London	Hewitt	Catworth	1	[illegible]			1	0
"	"	"	Brown	Dean	1	" "			1	0
"	"	"	Brown	Catworth	1	pkge			1	0

material is traced, isolated and listed, fascinating local historical happenings, often seasonal in nature, begin to emerge. Indeed, they highlight the huge changes that the station's opening must have brought about in the four years after 1866.

Local entrepreneurs would have changed the thinking on the supply of day-to-day provisions for Kimbolton and its surrounding villages. The latter would have been thriving farming communities still untouched by steam ploughs, threshing machines and other mechanisation.

Ploughs pulled by horses, and teams of men swishing scythes during the harvest, would still have been the classical scene in the farming calendar, even though new massive steam traction ploughs had been introduced in other parts of the country over ten years earlier. Within the next few years mechanisation, identified by coal supplies through the station for these steam ploughs, caused a huge rural depression with agricultural unemployment. This in turn led to people having to leave the area to seek work in the rapidly expanding industrial towns and cities on the coalfields, and estuarine ports on the coast.

The Granite and Slag Age

One striking feature in the delivery book related to large tonnages of slag and 'granite'. Each delivery had recorded against it the date of collection, the place of origin, the consignee, and the delivery address. The carter's name was duly signed in the book by either himself or, if he could not write, he placed a cross at the side of his name which was entered by the Midland Railway's goods agent as proof of release.

The appearance of the slag and 'granite' on such a vast scale was a surprise. During the period analysed forty one orders of slag were delivered to the station yard with a total weight of 718 tons 5 hundredweight (abbreviated as 'cwt'.). The average weight of each consignment was 17.5 tons with variations from 5.5 to over 31 tons.

Slag is the hot liquid waste product floated off the top of an iron or steel melt, at the end of each furnace process, which is then dumped in unsightly glass-like fragmentary heaps near the works. If the sulphur content is low the slag makes an ideal base for road and footpath construction.

The slag was shipped in from the ironworks at Wellingborough with an extra three from Thrapston and one fron Finedon. Wellingborough was developing into an important iron smelting centre while Thrapston was home to the Nene Side Iron Works which was supported by ironstone excavated from a quarry about a mile from the south-east edge of the town.

Half the orders were destined for T. Denton of Swineshead, a village a few miles to the south-west of Kimbolton. Mr. Manns (sometimes written as 'Mann'), from Brampton, near Huntingdon, came a close second. One of the carters of the slag, a Mr. Wiggins, must have realised that there was money to be made from this trade, and by the end of 1871 began to buy his own loads! All other orders, apart from those for Mr Denton, ended up in Kimbolton and Brampton and were often carried by men who could not write, hence the cross at the side of their name in the delivery book and the menial nature of their lives.

Mr. Denton did not appear on any of the local censuses at the time, so it may be assumed that he arrived specifically to deal with the sett-laying programme in the locality.

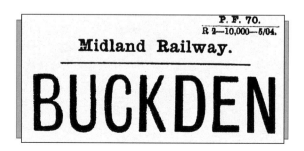

P. F. 70.
R 2—10,000—5/04.

Midland Railway.

BUCKDEN

At this time the village of Brampton was served by Buckden Station, (originally named 'Brampton' but changed to 'Buckden' on February 1st 1868), and was situated just one mile to the south. As the Brampton-bound slag was unloaded at Kimbolton, this may suggest that unloading facilities for such heavy unsavoury material (the lumps were glassy and sharp) were not available at Brampton in 1871.

Forty one loads of 'granite', totalling 475 tons 17cwt (average - 11.6 tons), were also received at Kimbolton during the same period. Mr. Denton again competed with other merchants for this market. The main receiver was Ellis & Everard, a company which still trades today under that name and whose history is explored briefly later due to its involvement in the early trading on the Midland Railway. Again Mr. Wiggins was the main carter, but Mr. Denton unloaded and carted his own orders.

Fig 21 - Ellis & Everard Private Wagon

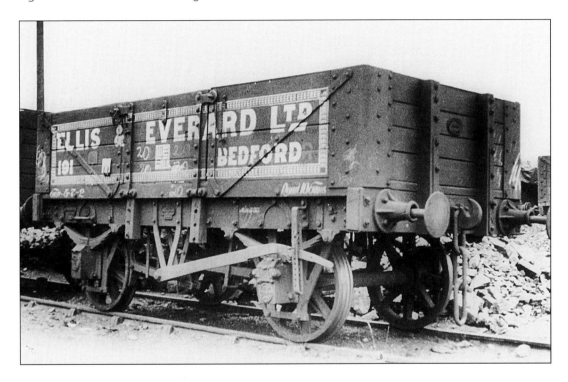

There were three 'granite' supply centres. All three quarries were located in a hilly area to the west of a line twelve miles long from Leicester north to Loughborough, and known as Charnwood Forest. This area is dominated by hard, durable 'granite', lava flows, volcanic dust and ancient sedimentary rocks of the Pre-Cambrian age, thus dating them at over six hundred million years old, and ideal for construction purposes. At the time it was the nearest such engineering stone to Kimbolton.

The first quarry, at Glenfield, was in the north-western suburbs of Leicester, adjacent to the village of Ratby and on the Leicester & Swannington Railway. The quarry, abandoned now, is sited near the M1 motorway. The second quarry is still operating at Bardon Hill, a couple of miles to the south east of Coalville in Leicestershire, and continues to generate rail-borne traffic today.

The third quarry, at Mountsorrel and also still operating, produces a pinkish granite-like variety of rock, but only one order came from here in 1871. This quarry was sited a short distance from the main Midland Railway line between Loughborough and Leicester. Apart from this single wagon-load the year's orders for 'granite', which arrived at Kimbolton Station, were equally divided between Bardon Hill and Glenfield quarries.

Ellis & Everard

It is worth dallying awhile over the affairs of this company. Its very origins were spawned by the growth of the railways back in the 1830's. The two Leicestershire men were farmers, Joseph Ellis from Glenfield and, in the next village, Breedon Everard from Groby. Joseph Ellis had many other irons in the fire. He was, in a small way, a maltster, and was also selling coal at Glenfield in 1830. He had associations with the founding of the Leicester & Swannington Railway which opened in 1832, and started selling coal through the stations on the Rugby and Birmingham lines from Leicester as soon as they opened for business.

Fig 22 - Joseph Ellis (1790-1857) and Breedon Everard (1814-1882)

The partnership between the two men began in 1848 when Joseph Ellis and Breedon Everard were employed by the Midland Railway Company to negotiate purchases of land for the new railway line from Syston to Peterborough, thus linking the latter city with Leicester. They were determined to be the leaders in selling coal at the new stations as soon as they were opened.

Breedon Everard had other business interests too. Before 1852, he was working a small granite quarry at Billa Barrow in Charnwood Forest. In that year, once more in partnership with Joseph Ellis, he opened a quarry at Markfield, and in 1857 he started the quarry at Bardon Hill where he later went to live.

The company grew into a highly successful outfit dealing in agricultural products, building materials, coal and coke. The commercial climate changed, however, as the decades rolled by, and Ellis & Everard decided to re-structure the company in the second half of the Twentieth Century, by discarding the old trappings, and they diverted their operations into chemical distribution services. This has been so successful they now own 41 companies in North America alone, in addition to the U.K. operation, and have expanded globally into Europe and the Far East to become the current fourth largest chemical distributor in the world. As I write, the company's independence has been brought into question due to a takeover bid from Holland.

Going back to Kimbolton, Ellis & Everard brought in sixteen orders for paving setts during 1871, all from Bardon Hill Quarry. One can see that the contract for the laying of the hard surface in Kimbolton town centre, from quarry to finished product, was finely interwoven between the Midland Railway and Ellis & Everard. The latter also had offices at Market Harborough, Kettering and Wellingborough, which were set up with the opening of the Bedford-Hitchin railway in 1857, and it was highly likely that this Kimbolton contract was handled through one of these offices.

Fig 23 - Ellis & Everard Market Harborough Office

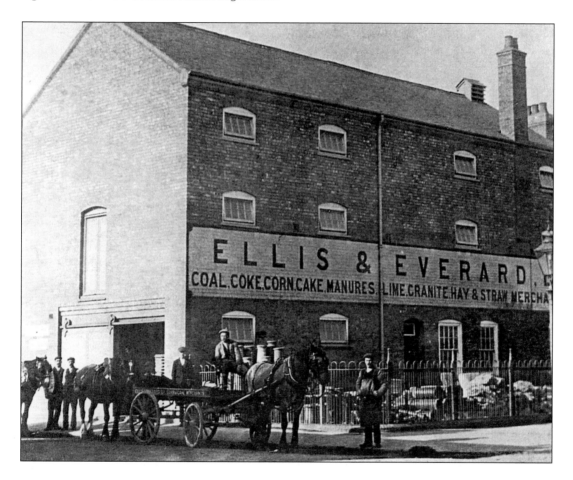

What was the "Granite"

I was intrigued by the word 'granite', so enquiries were made at the British Geological Survey centre near Nottingham where expert information was readily provided.

It was discovered that at Glenfield the word 'granite', which appeared in the 'Goods Delivery' book, was, in reality, a dark-grained igneous rock called diorite, sometimes varying to granodiorite. It is quite a decorative stone and was used for carving ancient Sumerian (Babylon) and Egyptian statues, bowls and vases.

The 'granite' from Bardon Hill was not true intrusive igneous granite but is given the mind-boggling description of porphyritic dacite, a darkish volcanic lava rock with larger (porphyritic) and smaller intermixed crystals of feldspar, whose origins were associated with a volcano. The quarry also contained dark andesitic tuffs (heat-welded volcanic ash composed of the igneous rock called andesite).

Armed with these descriptions a few enquiries resulted in tracking down a pile of loosely stacked 'granite' setts at a house called The Croft, Station Road, Tilbrook which is four miles west of Kimbolton. The sett illustrated in the accompanying photograph is a rough-sided rectangular block shaped by hammer and chisel, and is about 20 x 15 x 9 cms. in size. This example is composed of granodiorite and is likely to have come from Glenfield or Mountsorrel in this form. This sett has a fair amount of tar stuck to the worn traffic-smoothed surface suggesting that tarmacadam was laid on top at some stage in its later life before removal from a street or driveway.

A specimen of granodiorite was donated by Lafarge Redland, the building materials group, for this research. They own, and operate, the Mountsorrel Quarry and their specimen was geologically exactly the same as the sett from The Croft at Tilbrook.

Fig 24 - 'Granite' Sett from Tilbrook

It would be intriguing to know if anyone in the Kimbolton district ever saw kerbstones or setts in Kimbolton's High Street, Castle approach, driveways of country mansions, or surrounding village high streets, matching these descriptions. When they were replaced by tarmacadam in the early Twentieth Century, where were they dumped? Were they used on local farms? It is hoped that a fair amount of hammer tapping, a scrubbing of cobbles, and a scraping of overgrown rockeries will be heard in the locality in an attempt to locate more surviving setts from this episode in Kimbolton's history.

Local Agriculture

Before the arrival of the railway in 1866, local agriculture had to rely upon local resources, journeymen with horses and carts, crop rotation, and, as mentioned earlier, a small army of labourers to conduct the ploughing, sowing and harvesting cycle.

Dramatic changes were erupting in the New World and they were trickling down to affect daily life in Kimbolton. Not only was the rail network expanding, but further afield the North American Indians were being forced into reservations, and cattle barons in the same continent were reluctantly relinquishing their grasslands to be transformed into vast grain prairies. The recently designed clipper sailing ships were slashing the costs of transporting grain and other products to Europe.

In the Kimbolton area, where agriculture was dominated by pastoral activities coupled with a fair amount of arable, people involved with this new set of influences took advantage of the recently built railway. Its coming included telegraph facilities, and orders for these imported agricultural products sparked down the wires into the rapidly expanding ports from Kimbolton's local dealers and farmers. Exotic new feeds began to appear at Kimbolton Station. Even the fertility of the fields was not ignored, but more on that shortly.

The station was a major distribution centre for many villages within the locality. The villages named in the delivery book help identify the area served by the station and is called the hinterland. The accompanying map gives the reader some idea of the size of this area in 1871, which tended to stretch north-south due to the influences of Raunds and Grafham stations to the west and east respectively. The occasional load was bound for villages outside the hinterland but there must have been extenuating circumstances for this to occur.

It would seem that it did not take long for normally reticent farmers to be seduced by the benefits of the new cheaper feedstuffs. These included cotton seed cake, palm nut meal and maize from the New World. The feeds arriving from Europe were locust beans and tares (lentil-like vetch seeds), probably from the Mediterranean.

Imported wheat was not highly favoured, probably due to the presence of home grown supplies, and orders tended to be bought in the autumn from wholesalers in eastern England. One batch came from Kings Lynn and may have been imported from Denmark, which at this time was exporting large volumes of wheat, but was in the process of losing out to cheaper grain from the New World and the Russian steppes, thus depressing prices. This would have attracted farmers, always on the look-out for a bargain!

There was a reasonable range of British feeds used on the local farms. They were linseed cake, hog meal, white peas, oats, bran, turnips (one load only), barley, bone meal, middlings (coarse ground wheat) and 'corn'. These were mostly from suppliers within twenty miles of Kimbolton, but there seems to have been a major feed cake maker in Birmingham using linseed and cotton seed.

The imported materials arrived at a variety of ports including Victoria Docks (London), Birkenhead, Drypool (Hull), Waterloo Station, which was located in the northern Liverpool Docks area (and owned by the London & North Western Railway), and Boston. Canada was the source of one load of three tons of cotton cake (cotton is not grown in Canada; this load must have been bought from the USA by a Canadian agent).

Of the 214 cattle feed deliveries 57 per cent were ordered by Mr. TH Smith, the chief merchant of Tilbrook and the whole area. That village was much nearer the station than Kimbolton town and he took advantage of this proximity by building up a large wholesale business.

The port of Liverpool was often the source of linseed cakes. Linseed, from flax plants, was a very common crop in Ireland, the flax giving rise to their famous linen textile industry. The seeds were crushed for their oil, after being imported into Liverpool from Ireland, and the remaining crushed seed was processed into feed cake. Nothing was wasted.

Linseed cake blocks, according to the delivery book's very detailed records, were about seven pounds (3.2 kg) in weight, and cost £11.12s.6d (£11 52.5p) a ton in November, 1871, whereas the cotton seed cake blocks were about ten pounds (5kg) and retailed at the much lower price of only £6.2s.6d (£6 12.5p) a ton according to Ellis & Everard's catalogue prices at the time. The blocks were broken up by cake breakers, which were sold to farmers by the wholesaler Smith, who, in turn, ordered them for delivery via the station. The blocks were probably shaped like large thick circular discs because those imported through Waterloo Docks were marketed as 'Waterloo Rounds'.

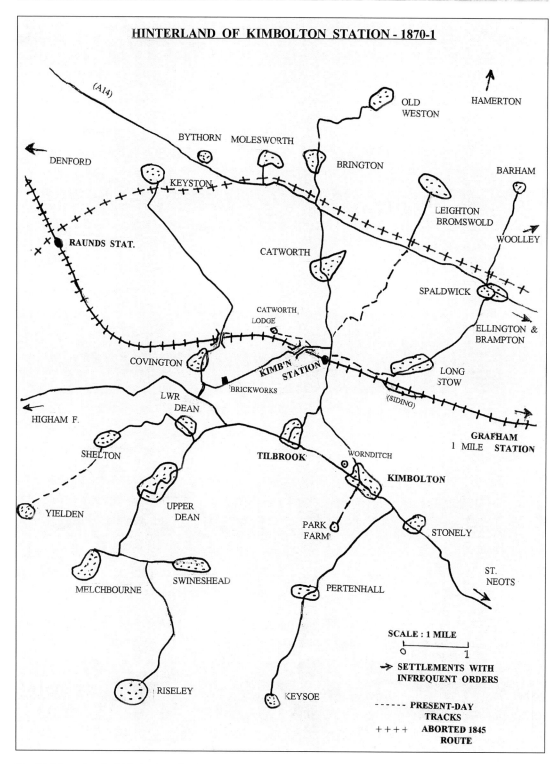

Fig 25 Hinterland of Kimbolton Station - 1870-71

Rape seed was delivered on two occasions in 1871. It has been suggested that rape oil, at the time, was inedible (even poisonous) for human consumption, until it was made safe by cross-breeding in the Twentieth Century. As these orders arrived in September the seeds were probably sown immediately, as in today's practice, and harvested in the following summer. Rape oil was used in the Nineteenth Century as horse liniment and domestic lighting oil.

Salt was used mainly for human consumption and food preservation. In November 1870 and April 1871 two deliveries totalling eleven tons arrived from Stoke-on-Trent, which is adjacent to the Cheshire Salt Field. Refrigeration was not invented until the 1880's, and was very expensive. The salt tonnage suggests that local needs were satisfied every half year by this size of order and Mr. Giddings of Kimbolton, was the trader.

Seed, for sowing, was an important trade. Most seeds were not specifically identified except for occasional loads of 'grass', and 'rye grass'. All these types of seeds were delivered between January and the end of April, for spring sowing. The other loads could well have been wheat, barley, oats and rye.

Farm Animal Arrivals

Throughout the year there was a steady trickle of animals arriving for local farms. These were solely from stations along the line between Kettering and Cambridge and consisted of sheep, pigs, 'beast' (cattle), one bull and even a gaggle of geese! Although the photograph below is not of Kimbolton it shows the sort of chaos a traveller may have encountered on a rural station's platform such as this one at Cockfield in Suffolk in 1900. The gaggle had just arrived at the station to be taken for fattening on Cockfield Great Green before being re-loaded at the station for the London market.

Fig 26 - A Gaggle of Geese about to be Loaded at Cockfield for London in 1900

Cattle Plague, also known as Rinderpest or Bovine Typhus

Three references in the 1866 log-book, on April 14, 26 and May 2nd, show that Kimbolton Station was notified by the Midland Railway's central office at Derby of the great Cattle Plague ravaging the British Isles at the time. This was at its height during 1865 and 1866 and suffered a total loss of 324,000 infected cattle. It was not finally eradicated until 1877.

Cattle Plague, or rinderpest, which, like foot-and-mouth, is caused by a virus, but one which is far more deadly. When cattle plague strikes a herd, up to nine out of ten animals may die in a new outbreak, although an immune build-up reduces the fatality rate to nearer 25 per cent if previous survivors become re-infected. The symptoms are similar to those of foot-and-mouth and are characterised by an ulcerative inflammation of the mucous membranes, especially those of the alimentary tract.

Cattle are most susceptible, and sheep and goats may occasionally become infected, although horses and pigs are immune. Cattle markets, pens, railway trucks, boats, or anywhere diseased cattle have been, are a source of contamination and thus help spread the disease.

The government of the day eventually introduced the Cattle Plague Bill in an attempt to deal with the disease, which first appeared in English herds in the last week of June 1865. The Bill included over forty clauses, most being passed unopposed, but some were contested vigorously during February 1866, just as Kimbolton Station, with its hinterland of pastoral farming, was about to open for business.

Clause 16 empowered local authorities to order the slaughter of healthy cattle, in addition to diseased ones, but only if they had been in contact with infected cases. An opposition amendment resisting this policy was heavily defeated after Disraeli supported the clause. This was the first occasion when a culling policy was introduced nationwide by central government during an outbreak of disease.

Culling was carried out by butchers travelling from farm to farm even though the risk of spreading the infection by this means was fully understood. The animals were brutally dispatched by means of a poleaxe to the neck, hence the reason for Clause 16 being known as the 'Poleaxe Clause'. The totally unskinned carcass then had to be buried on the same farm, thus potentially adding to the farmer's problems with tainted ground water.

Clauses 12 and 13 introduced the idea of compensation payments to the farmer whose herd had been slaughtered. The clause allowed up to £20 per animal to be paid, the final calculation being based on half the value of the animal. The compensation money would not come from central government, but would be raised by charging local people an extra rate of sixpence. So, the farmers found themselves paying an extra tax to receive compensation for their loss!

Clause 21 provided for the regulation of the movement of cattle. Mr Hunt introduced an amendment which asked for no movement of cattle by rail before March 25th, or along any highway, river or canal, except from field to field on the same farm to a maximum of 200 yards. Fears of a large increase in the price of meat and cheese (which indeed did occur) were expressed by opponents, but the clause was carried by 264 to 181 votes.

The whole Bill was passed on February 16th and was designed to remain in force until June 1st 1867. On Wednesday March 14th the House of Lords sent back amendments to include the withdrawal of the limiting of movement. This caused the whole Bill itself to be withdrawn. Another attempt to pass the Bill six days later was more agreeable to the Upper House. This allowed the movement of cattle after March 25th to a greater, but still limited, distance. The Government made an agreement with all railway companies that the Government would not inspect wagons, but passed the onus on to the railway companies to disinfect all wagons thoroughly. As you will see shortly, this turned out to be a loop-hole for malpractice.

On March 22nd London was re-infected by the disease by the illegal import of diseased cattle from Holland. The Plague was disappearing only slowly and fitfully in the country at large. Cumberland

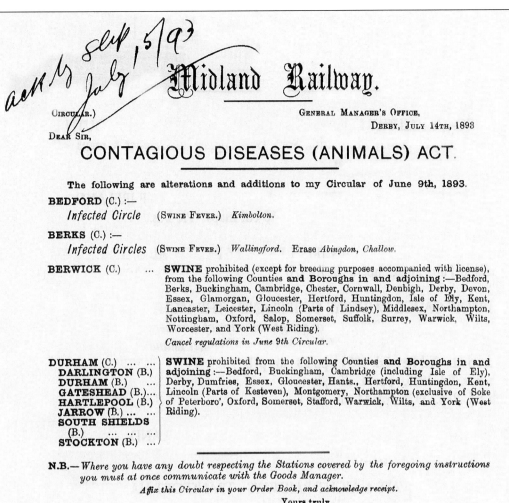

acted by Sept 15/93
July

Midland Railway.

(CIRCULAR.)

GENERAL MANAGER'S OFFICE,
DERBY, JULY 14TH, 1893

DEAR SIR,

CONTAGIOUS DISEASES (ANIMALS) ACT.

The following are alterations and additions to my Circular of June 9th, 1893.

BEDFORD (C.) :—

Infected Circle (SWINE FEVER.) *Kimbolton.*

BERKS (C.) :—

Infected Circles (SWINE FEVER.) *Wallingford.* Erase *Abingdon, Challow.*

BERWICK (C.) ... **SWINE** prohibited (except for breeding purposes accompanied with license), from the following Counties **and Boroughs in and adjoining** :—Bedford, Berks, Buckingham, Cambridge, Chester, Cornwall, Denbigh, Derby, Devon, Essex, Glamorgan, Gloucester, Hertford, Huntingdon, Isle of Ely, Kent, Lancaster, Leicester, Lincoln (Parts of Lindsey), Middlesex, Northampton, Nottingham, Oxford, Salop, Somerset, Suffolk, Surrey, Warwick, Wilts, Worcester, and York (West Riding).

Cancel regulations in June 9th Circular.

DURHAM (C.) ... ... **DARLINGTON** (B.) **DURHAM** (B.) ... **GATESHEAD** (B.)... **HARTLEPOOL** (B.) **JARROW** (B.) ... ... **SOUTH SHIELDS** (B.) ... ... **STOCKTON** (B.) ...	**SWINE** prohibited from the following Counties **and Boroughs in and adjoining** :—Bedford, Buckingham, Cambridge (including Isle of Ely), Derby, Dumfries, Essex, Gloucester, Hants., Hertford, Huntingdon, Kent, Lincoln (Parts of Kesteven), Montgomery, Northampton (exclusive of Soke of Peterboro'), Oxford, Somerset, Stafford, Warwick, Wilts, and York (West Riding).

N.B.—*Where you have any doubt respecting the Stations covered by the foregoing instructions you must at once communicate with the Goods Manager.*

Affix this Circular in your Order Book, and acknowledge receipt.

Yours truly,

GEO. H. TURNER,

GENERAL MANAGER.

Fig 27 - Example of Animal Movement Restriction Notice involving Kimbolton in 1893

and Cheshire were the main counties to be hit badly, although strangely, one of the only two counties not to suffer a single incident of the disease was Westmorland, adjacent to Cumberland (both now combined as Cumbria). The other was Monmouth. By mid-April the incidence of the Plague was on the decline, but herds were still being poleaxed. Cumberland was eventually free of the disease by the end of July 1866.

What attempts were made to treat the disease? In the middle of the Nineteenth Century conditions were rife for all manner of so-called 'remedies' to be tried by desperate farmers, and apparently there were plenty of Dickensian scallywags taking advantage of the situation. Vaccination was being used in 1866, with the injection of a liquid known as 'lymph', but this system was abused by charlatans. Another treatment was to administer a drink containing the chemical hyposulphate, but it acted merely as a purge which didn't help the comfort of the farmer in the daily management of the farmyard!

Probably the most effective treatment, whose success rate was discussed in Parliament a great deal, was the 'Diet of Worms'. It wasn't what you immediately think! It was a remedy introduced by a gentleman farmer called Mr Worms who returned with the details of the concoction from Ceylon, now known as Sri Lanka. The mixture fed to cattle included:-

1 lb of red pickling onions and 1 lb of garlic. Peel both, place in a mortar and pound to a pulp. To the pulp add a lb of ground ginger, and mix thoroughly.

Take 3/4 lb of Assafoetida (foetid fungus) - add water to cover it, boil until no sediment remains, then remove all residual solids. Pour the resultant liquid over the onion, garlic and ginger pulp and stir thoroughly.

Add 2 gallons of rice-water, then allow to cool. Administer to the cattle.

This treatment was used on two illustrious estates, namely Stoneleigh Abbey and Mentmore, the latter belonging to Baron de Rothschild no less. Both estates reported that all infected cattle were cured!

Another treatment of the disease was undertaken by means of administering what was described at the time as "Homeopathic Tincture of Arsenic". Annual production of this poison in the Nineteenth Century ran into thousands of tons from the tin mines in Devon and Cornwall. It begs the question as to whether the meat from treated cattle eventually found its way into human beef supplies. A typical advertisement of the time, from the St Neots Chronicle, is seen below:-

Fig 28 - Cattle Plague Treatment Advertisement 1866

THE ARSENIC TREATMENT

(*Homœopathic*)

OF THE CATTLE PLAGUE.

PREVENTIVE MEDICINE:—the Homœopathic Tincture of Arsenic—now being adopted as a preventive to the above Disease, can be had thus:—

A Supply for 3 Beasts for a Month, 2s. 6d.
" 6 " " 4s. 6d.
" 20 " " 10s. 6d.

Treatment of an Attack:—A complete set of Tinctures (Six) used in the treatment of an attack, with full directions for use and for action in every emergency, 9s., 15s., 26s., 42s., and 66s., according to the number of Cattle to be treated. They are supplied and well-arranged in deal boxes.

The above Medicines are prepared by JAMES EPPS, Homœopathic Chemist, (the first established in England 112, Great Russell Street; 170, Piccadilly; and 48, Threadneedle Street, London; and each Bottle is secured by a band over the cork, bearing his signature, without which none are genuine.

Sole Agent for St. Neots:—

J. ELGER, Ornamental Hair Manufacturer and Perfumer, High Street.

Local committees were set up to deal with any applications to move cattle by rail. The General Quarter Sessions of the Peace held at Shire Hall in Huntingdon, under the watchful heavyweights the Earl of Sandwich and the Duke of Manchester, tried to keep a wary eye on local conditions and issued licenses for the movement of animals, hay and fodder within the county of Huntingdonshire.

One incident of illegal movement, in another county, was taken before Horncastle, Lincolnshire Petty Sessions, and it involved a Mr Stanhope of Revesby being accused of moving two cows and sixteen bullocks to Tattershall, without permission, along a public highway towards the nearest Great Northern Railway station. This case generated much excitement and media interest, and the court proceedings lasted six hours. Mr Stanhope was fined 20 shillings with costs. All this, like the foot-and-mouth epidemic of 2001, must have caused much disruption and hit the operating profits of the railway companies hard. Farm animals and manure were still being transported from and to Kimbolton Station at the same time as the plague notifications were being received (see Appendix 1), presumably under local licence.

This great plague brought about an important development for future responses to such outbreaks. It caused the railway companies to issue a series of notices and orders, which eventually evolved into booklets entitled "Cattle Disease", or the "C.D. Booklet", around 1887 and thereafter.

In 1866, Bedfordshire was receiving large quantities of manure from London by train for use on the land. On February 3rd of that year Justices of the Peace in the county were informed that parts of dead animals were believed to have been mixed in with the manure and there was fear of the spread of the cattle plague. Not only were the farmers concerned but it would appear there was some disagreement between the three Bedfordshire railway companies over the way this problem should be addressed effectively. The three companies were the Great Northern Railway, the Midland Railway, and the London & North Western Railway.

The Great Northern Railway representative believed that only horse manure was being sent from London because the company employed a man to see that no carcasses were included. The company required a certificate, issued by the senders of the manure and signed by the Metropolitan Inspectors, be used as a regulatory control. Failing the existence of a certificate the company would refuse to transport manure from sources suspected of being contaminated.

The Midland Railway agreed likewise but the London & North Western Railway did not comply at this time, and as a result were likely to be called before the Court. A few days later, in late February, a farmer and a London & North Western Railway clerk appeared in court for permitting livestock movement between Buckinghamshire (an infected county) and Bedfordshire on the Bletchley to Bedford line, without permission.

An immediate ban was imposed on the movement of farm animals, raw or untanned hide, skin, hoof, offal and bones into the county from any part of Great Britain. Similarly, movement was restricted until March 1st 1866, within the confines of Bedford county, on the transport of hay, straw, manure, fodder and litter "likely to propagate infection" from places where the disease existed within the previous 42 days. The restriction also applied to the movement of sheep, lambs, goats and pigs within the same county.

It is interesting to note that Huntingdonshire used a shorter restriction period of 28 days after a previous incident of the plague, and before movements were allowed once more, thus showing how piecemeal the regulations were at the time. Despite all the culling and movement restrictions, and the classic rise and fall of the plague over the course of the first year, the infection continued to re-appear in isolated incidents for several years before finally being eradicated in 1877, twelve years after it first burst upon the agricultural scene.

Preventative regulations have been shown to be so much tighter in the 2001 foot-and mouth plague after 135 years of centralising and honing 'fire engine' action plans - aren't they? I do apologise for my mild sense of humour if you feel it is not suitable!

"Ignore history at your peril" and "if you don't know your history you don't know where you're going" are two sayings that spring to mind.

Although this section is not directly related to the detailed history of Kimbolton Station, it does give a very clear picture of the prevailing agricultural and associated commercial conditions which reached crisis point in the very month when Kimbolton Station was being prepared for the official opening. It was anticipated that the farm animal trade was going to be a significant revenue generator for the station, and the plague did have an influence on livestock shipments from the goods yard. As you will see in a later section, farm animal movements did become an important facet of the station's daily life.

A Very Smelly Station

"Be careful where you tread, sir" must have been a common opening gambit at Kimbolton Station. Huge loads of fertilizer were delivered to the goods yard by rail. It was somewhat surprising to discover how much fertilizer was needed to maintain soil fertility even though there were large numbers of animals on the local farms. The fertilizer arrived in three forms.

By far the largest volume of fertilizer type was horse manure. The second form was from Bramford, on the outskirts of Ipswich. This settlement was the base for processing coprolites into fertilizer powder. Coprolites were found in huge accumulations, and especially in the area between Cambridge and Gamlingay, fifteen miles to the west of the former settlement, in the mid-Nineteenth Century, and were quarried for this commercial purpose!

Fig 29 - Coprolite Train leaving Whaddon Pit , South Cambridgeshire en route for Meldreth Station Goods Yard in 1880

The exploitation of coprolite helped establish a company called Fisons. The material was often concentrated on site then transported to either one of the six small factories dotted around Cambridge and Royston, or one of four in Ipswich, whose products contributed to the export trade. There is even a street in Ipswich called "Coprolite Street" to commemorate this trade.

Coprolite is a term applied more to those masses of phosphate found in sedimentary rocks which exhibit a corrugated or convoluted form corresponding to what were the forms of the internal casts of the intestines of certain fishes, dinosaurs and dolphin-like reptilian sea creatures. This material included their excrement, as in the very realistic accompanying photograph of such an example from a large dog-sized dinosaur (it contains fragments of sea urchin), which was 'deposited' on an ancient seashore 120 million years ago in the Jurassic. This specimen was found, appropriately, near the Midland Railway in Sharnbrook, Bedfordshire.

Thirdly, a new form of 'super' fertilizer was delivered to the district at this time, aided by the arrival of the railway. It was called guano. The first delivery, of five tons, occurred on March 31st 1866. Guano was composed essentially of seabird droppings that had been recently discovered plastered

Fig 30 - Fison's Letterhead (1868) Advertising Coprolites with Recently Excavated Sample

thickly over the tops of small offshore islands and sea stacks off the coasts of Peru and Ecuador in western South America. The acidic droppings chemically combined with the limestone rock underneath to form a superb fertilizer, calcium phosphate. The cold offshore Peruvian Ocean Current encourages the build-up of huge shoals of anchovies which support enormous numbers of fish-guzzling cormorants and pelicans. These reside upon the islands, hence the guano.

For thousands of years droppings built up to ten to fifteen metres in thickness. They were laboriously quarried by hand, bagged and transported via the Magellan Straits, in sailing ships, for spreading on the fields of Britain. The Onedin Line, from Birkenhead, was one company involved in this trade, and, as the Kimbolton guano was imported through this port, Onedin could well have been the company, made famous by a television series, which transported this smell-at-two-miles-distance material.

The guano was marketed in the United Kingdom by Messrs. L Thomson, T Bonar & Company. They were appointed as sole consignees and agents by the Peruvian Government. As you can see from the newspaper advertisement below the minimum quantity of guano sold per order by Thomson & Bonar was 30 tons, so TH Smith's orders, for 10.5 and 5 tons respectively, must have come from an intermediate agent. With percentages being added at each handling this must have made the commodity rather expensive.

Fig 31 - Guano Advertisement in the St Neots Chronicle, February 1866

PERUVIAN GOVERNMENT GUANO.

L. THOMSON, T. BONAR & Co.,

57¼ OLD BROAD STREET LONDON, E.C.

SOLE CONSIGNEES AND AGENTS FOR SALE IN GREAT BRITAIN & IRELAND

Price at Scale in London, fixed by the Peruvian Government. £12 *per Ton for quantities of not less than 30 Tons.*

FEBRUARY, 1866.

Only two loads of guano were bought during 1871, both by Mr TH Smith of Tilbrook, but they represented a significant feature in the evolution of the area's commerce. Guano must have been expensive, due to the transport costs when compared with manure, but it was magnificent stuff. So, a little of the Pacific Ocean found its way to Kimbolton along the Midland Railway line.

The total inflow of fertilizer, for the year, was 134.5 tons. Manure accounted for 87 tons, coprolites 32 and guano 15.5 tons. Manure was usually in bagged loads totalling from one to six tons, coprolites up to ten tons and guano arrived in five or ten ton loads.

As mentioned earlier manure was bought from dealers in towns and cities where the horse was still king of transport. Kimbolton received large supplies from Birmingham, and Huntingdon (where it was received from London via the Great Northern Railway on a regular daily service known as the 'Dung Train'). In 1871 one load came from Wolverhampton. Eleven orders came direct from London, most being identified as originating from Blackwall. This must have been an excellent method of ridding the capital of its huge steaming heaps. Small-time village manure agents, often farmers looking for secondary income, would buy supplies from larger city dealers, then sell on to other local farmers. Such a chain of contracts can be seen in the following letter-headings:-

Fig 32 - Letterheads for Local Farmers

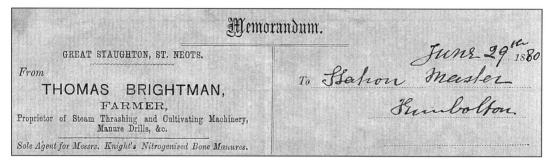

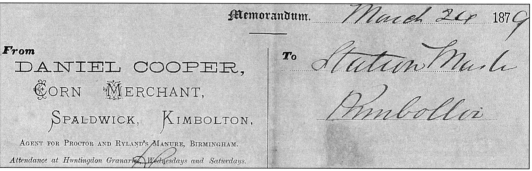

Two unusual orders of manure arrived from London (6 tons & 3 tons) for Mr. Fuller of Ramsey, 25 miles to the east. Were they transported by cart to Ramsey or was the manure used on local Kimbolton farms owned by Mr. Fuller?

Fertilizer was a very seasonal trade. The months of February, March (especially) and April saw all but one, out of 49 deliveries, arrive. These springtime deliveries were presumably for the summer growing season for grass leys and arable crops.

Pollards

Today, people accept plastic bags, pallets and containers as the norm. In 1870 wicker baskets and jute bags were the main containers. The baskets were woven out of very long, thin, lithe twigs, called pollards, which were cut from osier beds. These were maintained low-lying areas of willow trees, kept almost to ground level, from which grew long slender stems. These pollards would bend relatively easily as they were woven into wickerwork baskets, which were used in the home, shops and on the farm for storage. Vast numbers were needed at the time for a wide range of jobs.

The nearest osier beds to Kimbolton were in the Great Ouse valley in the Huntingdon area, and it was a quick, easy journey from Huntingdon East Station to Kimbolton Station. During 1871 fourteen

Midland Railway.

HUNTINGDON

orders were delivered to the station. Half were for Mr. Spicer, merchant, of East Street, Kimbolton, and six were for Mr. Smith of Tilbrook. The odd lot was bought by Mr. Chapman of Wornditch, just outside Kimbolton on the Tilbrook side. The orders were of considerable size; most were of two tons in weight, but varied from one to five and a quarter tons. This poses the question - did the wholesalers make baskets or did they sell the pollards to individuals to construct their own?

Eat and be Merry

Very little identifiable food came in by rail. As suggested earlier, it most likely arrived in the large number of containers called 'hampers'. Non-perishable deliveries were flour and cheese.

The flour trade was cornered totally by Mr. Smith of Tilbrook. Even so, the amount received was not considerable in volume, for there was a windmill west of Tilbrook, and Mr Mehew, owner of Kimbolton Mill, took care of the local town demand. Only seven orders were received at the station over the year, five coming from Huntingdon and two from St. Ives. The flour came in sacks each weighing 2 cwt 2 quarters (127 kg). One transhipment note shows that Mr. Smith was asked to forward a Rev. Young's wheat (ten quarters) to the magnificent, and recently renovated river mill at Houghton near St. Ives.

There were probably large numbers of dairy cattle in the district, giving rise to local cheese-making, which was supported by other cheeses bought in by Mr. Hollis of Catworth. This gentleman must have been the local cheese expert. A total of only four orders were delivered in the year, in boxes totalling 206 pounds in weight, and they arrived in June, July and August. All the cheese came from Huntingdon.

The locals loved their wine! There is no doubt about that. The station served the community well, but not one order was for Kimbolton. Does this mean that the 'townees' were teetotal or did they still receive their tipples through road deliveries? All the wine orders went to the surrounding villages in boxes, hampers and cases weighing about one hundredweight each. The wine came from suppliers in Northampton, Market Harborough, London and Leicester in the main.

Ale, Stout, Spirits, Hops & Tobacco

The considerable amount of alcohol delivered to the station was for consumption around the whole district. Kimbolton town's thirst was quenched by locally brewed beer in 1871. Information on this topic has been gratefully provided by Keith Osborne of Wellingborough. He has written a book entitled "The Brewers of Cromwell's County", which was published in December 1999.

There were three brewers in Kimbolton in 1870, the first being Hensman, in Clancarty House. The other two were run by members of the Hatfield family. Their main brewery was only two doors away from Hensman's, and the beer was sold in their pub called the Black Swan, now a pharmacy sporting the same name. This brewery lasted until the 1880's. The family's other brew-house was run by Thomas Hatfield. A brewery was to be found also in Stonely, a mile along the main road to the east of the town.

All this helps explain why beer imported through the station was mainly destined for the local villages rather than Kimbolton. Out of 28 orders for ale and stout, nine ended up in Catworth, four each in Molesworth (Mr. Cave) and Covington (Mr. Watson), three in Dean (Mr. Campion) and two in Tilbrook (T. Smith). This may give a clue as to which villages had their own brewhouses. Mr. Pashler seems to have been a buyer, delivering to Catworth, Molesworth, and once only to Kimbolton.

All the brewing in Kimbolton would have needed hops, but only two orders arrived by rail in 1871. The second was only a small 28 pound bag, bound for Mr Pashler, but the first, in February, was bought by TH Smith of Tilbrook and weighed a massive two and a third tons! Did the Kimbolton brewers buy their hops from this merchant or were they still receiving them from other sources, rumbling up the road from St. Neots Station direct from London and Kent, the main hop growing area. The following letterhead came from the "Beer at home means Davenports" stable, and was on a letter to Kimbolton Station. Remember the television advert jingle?

Fig 33 - Davenport the Hop Supplier

The brews came from centres which were served by the Midland Railway again. The beer travelled in firkins (9 gallon, or 40 litre, barrels) and kilners, which were huge jars with air-tight lids for preservation. The brewery suppliers were from Wellingborough, Thrapston (supplier only, not a brewery), and Kettering, while one dealer, Mr. Watson, tickled the local palates with top-quality beer from the famed breweries of Burton-on-Trent. One of these Burton deliveries was destined for Kimbolton, adding a little competition to the town's brewers.

Spirits were popular in the district, but only four jars arrived in the summer. Each jar weighed from 65 pounds to one hundredweight. Brandy was bought by Mr. Harris of Kimbolton. At the time cognac was about £1.35, whisky 85p and gin a mere 45p a gallon!

Only one load of tobacco arrived. This came from St. Pancras for Mr B Clarke of Kimbolton, in a box weighing 56 pounds. Again, was some of this product still coming in by road? The railway was only four years old, and some people may have been using their old suppliers in places like St. Neots and carting them to Kimbolton.

Let Them Eat Cake - then Wash Afterwards

Cakes may have been popular, but for those special occasions confectionery was bought from Leicester by the Tebbs family of Catworth. During the year, two chests of confectionery arrived, in August and September. The weight of each chest was one hundredweight and 1.3 hundredweight respectively. These weights included the chests but they were still considerable orders.

Kimbolton was quite a clean-living place, for over half a ton of soap arrived in two lots in March 1871. One came from Wakefield for Mr Abbott who lived in Old Weston. He dealt in clothes so he probably used the soap for washing the items before selling them. The other order was for Mr T Smith of Tilbrook and came from a London supplier.

Fig 34 - Allsopp's Brewery, Burton-on-Trent on the Midland Railway, 1866.

High Fashion

People would have made their own clothes to some degree but there was a surprisingly large trade with 69 bundles of clothes passing through the station to a wide variety of local traders. Each bundle weighed half a hundredweight. The heaviest month for deliveries was October, presumably for winter body protection.

The main clothing wholesaler was Mr Brown, of Dean, but he also had a depot at Catworth. He was responsible for nearly half the year's orders arriving at the station. Catworth seems to have been a major clothing distribution centre with Messrs. Whitney and Hewitt also conducting business there.

About a quarter of all orders were for individuals in a variety of local villages, but only one order was for Kimbolton. Does this mean that yet another commodity was still making its way into the town by road?

All the clothes orders came in from London, presumably via St. Pancras. This is a remarkable feature considering the Midland Railway was also directly linked to the internationally important cotton and woollen textile manufacturing centres of Manchester and Leeds. There was a wide variety of buyers using the London market. Only one delivery of leather occurred, in October 1871, for Mr J Coales of Leighton Bromswold, which weighed nearly ninety pounds.

Furniture was probably made locally, unless the pieces came in by road. Only two lots came in by rail, one of which was for the Duke of Manchester. This included fifty packages weighing a total of one ton. The other order was for Mr Chattell of Leighton Bromswold and only weighed 3.5 hundredweight.

Industry

There were a few aspects to this topic that came to light. The first kept the wheels of society turning. When one considers the amount of grease needed for axles at the time very little was delivered to the station. Only one load was ordered by Mr. Spriggs. This name appears quite frequently in the delivery book, and it is usually involved with the station, where he was listed as the "Agent". He could well have been the station-master or the Midland Railway Company's goods agent. Was the grease for rail and road wagon axle boxes? Only two barrels of oil appeared, for Mr Giddings of Kimbolton, the salt merchant and grocer.

The Coal Trade and Related Industry

Railways were originally built to transport minerals, particularly coal. The Midland Railway was desperate to expand its influence in the London domestic market for coal, and, as already described, this feature played a large part in the decision to build the extension from Bedford to St Pancras. As a result of the Industrial Revolution forests were, by now, sadly depleted, and the introduction of coal as a heating fuel in urban centres was a blessing.

There have been a few surprises in this study so far, but another two were lurking around 'King Coal'. First, Kimbolton Station's goods agent only registered the arrival of one order for this fuel through the goods yard in the whole of 1871 and that was for Mr. Holmes, of Catworth, in late springtime, too late for the winter freeze! The coal came from a merchant in Thrapston, was about 3.5 tons in weight, and was presumably for private purposes.

Clark's the coal merchants were either attracting no business at all or they had separate goods delivery books from those operated by the station. Even Thomas Smith, the largest wholesaler in the district, did not have his own business goods delivery books until much later in the decade.

A Lot of Gas in Kimbolton

The second surprise also involved energy supplies. How did the rest of the locals keep warm? There must have been a large amount of wood still being cut, and it was cheaper and more accessible. However, there certainly was coal in Kimbolton at this time because it was discovered that two consignments of iron and distillation retorts were for the Kimbolton Gas Company! Considering this very small town's isolated situation and a total lack of Victorian industrial stimulation of population growth, the existence of such an undertaking was a revelation.

Fig 35 - An Aerial photograph of Kimbolton Gasworks in the 1930's

The gasworks existed from 1854 to 1939, stood in the garden of what is now the "Mason", a house in Carnaby and boasted two gasholders. George Bower of St. Neots, famed for his inventions of gas meters, gas cookers and gas lighting in railway carriages, was expanding his gas industry at the end of Fisher's Yard at the back of the Market Square in St Neots. He found ready sales, even as far afield as Argentina, and was responsible for installing the gas lighting in the palace of the Viceroy of Egypt. Was Kimbolton Castle lit by gas supplied by the Kimbolton Gasworks at some stage, I wonder?

It was in 1852 that Bower bought out the Kimbolton ironmonger called Braybrook. With this toe-hold in the town he built the gasworks in 1854, situated behind the church. It is not known whether he was also the investor or merely the engineer, for no records of the gas company exist in the Huntingdon Record Office.

The gasworks required coal deliveries for twelve years before the railway was built, so coal must have been received by other means. Bower's direct involvement in the company probably meant that the coal was carted in from the start in 1854 through the Great Northern Railway's station at St.

Fig 36 - 25" Scale 1902 O.S. Map of Kimbolton Showing Gasworks

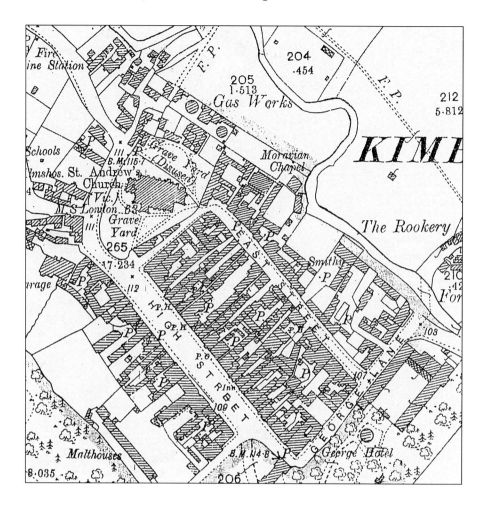

Neots. Evidence for a coal handling facility at the station was found in an 1855 edition of the St. Neots Chronicle:-

By Appointment
CHRISTOPHER HALL
COAL AGENT
TO THE GREAT NORTHERN RAILWAY

Orders given and received at the OFFICE, CAMBRIDGE STREET, ST. NEOTS, for COALS, at the Station Prices, viz. :-

	s. d.
Walls End	19 0 per ton.
Best Silkstone	16 0 "
Derby Soft	15 0 "
Hard Coal	15 0 "
Soft ditto	14 0 "

Good Slack, suitable for stoves and close fires..14 0 sh. per ton
Carted to any part of the Town for Two Shillings per ton extra, for Cash only.

Present Retail Prices at the Yard, viz :-

	s. d.
Walls End	1 1 per cwt.
Best Silkstone	1 0 "
Hard Coal	0 11 "
Soft ditto	0 10 "
Good Slack	0 10 "

According to Mott and Awdry 3,500 tons of coal were being handled annually at Kimbolton Station by the mid-1870's. Compare that with 1871. The gasworks may have changed its coal delivery patterns. The local people may have suddenly discovered coal for their domestic fires.

The origins of the coal were identified easily because it was retailed under the name of the coal seam from which it was mined, and thus provided the customer with information about its quality. Coal in the advertisement above came from Derbyshire (Hard and Soft Coals), West Yorkshire (Silkstone Coal) and Northumberland (Walls End Coal). All were excellent for gas and coke-making.

The gentleman who operated the coal sales business from Kimbolton by 1884 was Benjamin Measures who lived at Tilbrook Grange next door to the station. The following illustration shows that some of the coal came from Wombwell Main Colliery, a few miles to the south of Barnsley, again on the Midland Railway, and so could be handled by the company throughout its journey.

Once the coal order in the illustration below had arrived at the station it was transported down the hill for Mr Copland in Kimbolton. This suggests that either the Clark & Company coal merchants business had not been that successful or Mr Measures had become a competitor. The lack of identifiable orders related to Clark in any earlier deliveries suggests the former and they had withdrawn from the scene.

KIMBOLTON STATION,

Jan 7 1885

Mr. A Copland Kimbolton

Bought of BENJAMIN MEASURES.

If paid for within One Month 1s. per Ton Discount will be allowed.

	WEIGHT. TON.	CWT.	QRS.	RATE	AMOUNT. £.	s.	d.
Wombwell Main							
Best Brights							
" Main Screened		6	0				
" Hard							
" Purified Coke							
Carting							

Carter's Name

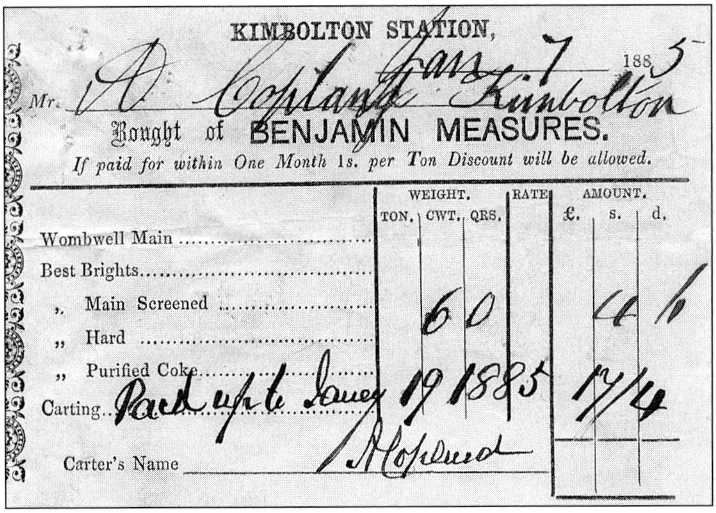

Fig 37 - Kimbolton Station's coal merchant in 1884

If I allow myself to be slightly side-tracked at this point now that the settlement of Barnsley has been mentioned, loyalty and ease of passage often led to a passenger purchasing a ticket that was routed throughout by the same company. An example is illustrated below which shows a journey from Cambridge (where the Midland had an office) to Barnsley in 1904.

The shortest route would have involved three separate companies via the East Coast Main Line but, as you can see, the person was sent on one train to Kettering, via Kimbolton, where he would have changed for Sheffield. He would have caught another train from Sheffield to Barnsley thus ensuring all sections of the journey being operated by the Midland Railway.

Fig 38 - Cambridge to Barnsley via Kimbolton in 1904

Odds and Ends

Five loads of pipes were received for people in Kimbolton (Love), Pertenhall (Martyn), Tilbrook (Rawlins) and Swineshead (Denton). One load was 2.5 tons in weight and consisted of 640 pipes, thus making each one a mere nine pounds in weight. This strongly suggests clay pipes. These may have been for sewerage drains which were being constructed for the first time all over the country. Whatever they were, they originated from Woodville, a suburb of Swadlincote, in South East Derbyshire, where there were copious supplies of clay.

Ropes and string were fairly regular arrivals; all but one delivery, were for Kimbolton Station's agent. These came from the Midland Railway centres at Burton-on-Trent, Leicester, London and Trent Junction, an isolated station half way between Derby and Nottingham, next to which the Midland Railway's sheet stores were situated. It was such a bleak location that the local children used to recite, in school assembly, the Lord's Prayer: "And lead us not into Trent Station"!

The coming of the railway was a boon to local builders. Timber was bought from dealers in Wisbech (spelt 'Wisbeach' in the 19th Century), Peterborough and London. Deal was the main wood type used by the building trade at the time. Columns, ventilators, skylights, fencing, window frames and various bits of building equipment arrived from all over the Midlands, and showed that the local builders were taking advantage of new sources of mass production. Cases of glass also arrived at the station. Two loads of scantling were delivered, these being thin, narrow strips of wood used for fixing tiles to roofs.

No bricks were delivered to the station in 1871, probably because there was a fairly local brickworks, near Kimbolton Station, which quarried the Oxford Clay on site. Today it is totally overgrown and is on the north side of the back road from Covington to Tilbrook Grange. It was known as the 'Catworth Tile & Brick Company'.

Only one order for bricks, in all the books analysed, was unearthed and that was on June 24th, 1866 for a load from Ellis & Co. in Coalville, Leicestershire. This company was owned by Mr Ellis, of Ellis & Everard.

"Any Old Iron"

A great surprise was the appearance of iron ore in the delivery book. The closest long-life ore field was at Thrapston, but the nearest that iron ore quarrying crept towards Kimbolton was at Raunds, eight miles to the west. That operation did not sprout until 1879 but, because of the poor quality of the ore, closed down only two years later. So, why were two separate loads of iron ore being delivered to Kimbolton Station in 1871?

The first load came on June 24th from Wellingborough where there was a good quality Jurassic sedimentary iron ore field. This 11 tons 6 cwt. load was ordered by Mr. T Denton, from the small village of Swineshead. Average iron content of these local ores was about 20 per cent so, at best, the smelt could not have extracted more than three tons of iron metal. Was the ore heading for a puddle furnace in Swineshead or was it for a blacksmith?

The second load, a month later, was destined for Mr. Mann of Brampton. Does this mean that Buckden Station could not handle such a load? This adds more evidence to the suggestion that a siding facility for handling such material was not yet installed at Buckden in 1871. This was probably the case when you are introduced to a discussion on a Mr Golightly's activities shortly.

This second load was 25 tons 3 cwt. suggesting a potential smelt of about six tons of iron metal. Mr. Mann was a small dealer in slag and 'granite', also through Kimbolton Station, so he could have been the local Brampton merchant in primary materials. He may have even dabbled in a small puddling furnace.

The Duke of Manchester

Residing at the castle, the Duke seems to have used the station's goods facilities only sparingly during 1871. On consignment notes and in the 'Goods Delivery' book he was usually identified as the "Duke" or "Manchester", and the orders were for iron troughs, other iron products and furniture. The iron materials always came from Belfast and, as that city was to the west, there was a likelihood he had no option but to swallow his pride and use the Midland Railway services. Did the Duke have vested interests over the water? The question is asked because pig iron had to be brought into Belfast from England for their local industries.

Fig 39 - Duke of Manchester's Patronage of the Station

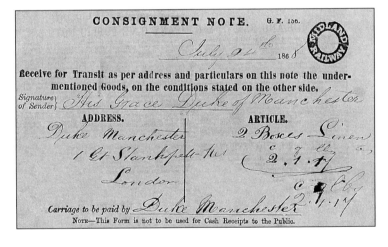

The 1866 log-book registers many journeys undertaken by men belonging to the 'Volunteer Movement'. This was a forerunner of the Territorial Army and first came into existence in 1861. The Duke of Manchester's 1st Huntingdonshire Light Horse section was regarded, for years, as the finest cavalry regiment in the Volunteer Service in England. The arrival of the railway was a tremendous boost for such an outfit where efficiency of movement was essential, and the log-book shows that the local station was used frequently by the volunteers for regimental business.

Although the Duke and the Railway Company co-operated well in the very early years during the spawning of the line, the Duke, like certain other landowners, seems to have treated the organisation as if it were there for his personal benefit. According to the exhaustive and detailed researches of John Rhodes ('The Kettering-Huntingdon Line' booklet) the 1866 timetable did not generate the anticipated passenger revenue for the railway company, so the trains were re-scheduled. This had a most positive effect financially for the Company (it doubled the revenue!), but it really upset the man residing in his castle!

The Duke coerced the Earl of Sandwich, who lived at Hinchingbrooke House, Huntingdon, into supporting him in an attempt to retain certain trains from the old timetable. When this was denied to them, letters began to flow between the two parties. The Duke began to insist that trains should be stopped at Kimbolton on demand, but this was skilfully resisted by the Midland Railway secretary.

Fig 40 - Huntingdonshire Volunteers on Parade at Kimbolton Castle

This may be a probable explanation as to why there was an enormous reduction in the Duke's patronage of Kimbolton Station between 1868 and 1871.

The differences in timing between the March1866 timetable and the 1870 signal-box register can be found in Appendix 3. The latter also highlights how unreliable the punctuality of trains could be on sample working days. This may well have added to the Duke of Manchester's gripes at the time.

Empty Sacks and Hampers

An area's commerce was conducted successfully with the aid of huge jute sacks in which manufactured, processed and raw agricultural materials could be transported. During the year 1208 bundles of empty sacks came into the station to aid the movement of such materials. Only on a few occasions were the weights of the bundles shown, their average being about one hundredweight.

The main supplies came from that place of blessed reputation, Trent Junction (53%). Next came Huntingdon (18%), then Wellingborough (7%), Birmingham (5%) and smaller numbers from Kettering, Atherstone and St. Ives. These were all Midland Railway locations again, or close by. The sacks were either the property of the Midland Railway Company, and identified in the delivery book as ordered by the "Agent", or were privately owned.

Mr Golightly's Ghost Train

Early in 1871 some rather different commodities arrived at Kimbolton Station in the form of railway materials. They formed a complete set of railway building materials! Rails, sleepers, chairs, spikes, fishplates and bolts, slag for the track base, and fencing. The total number of sleepers and the weights

Fig 41 - Kimbolton's Midland Railway feeder network, 1870

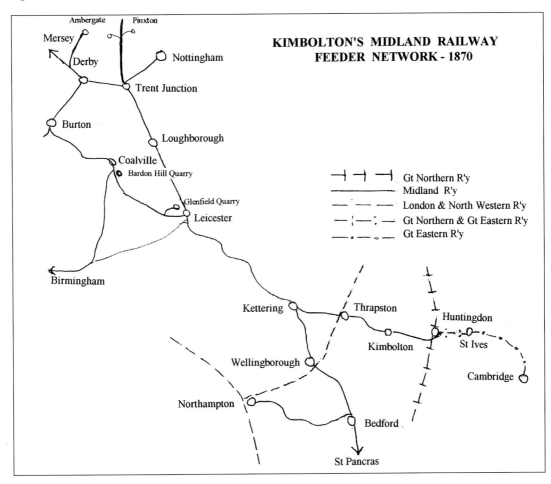

of material, strongly suggests that Mr Golightly, the consignee, was contemplating laying about a mile of standard gauge railway line in the locality. But where?

Fig 42 - Track Components

The sleepers were each about one hundredweight in weight and the rails were 4.1 hundredweight. It was only in the 1870's that steel began to replace iron as the rail-making material. This was ten times more durable, but

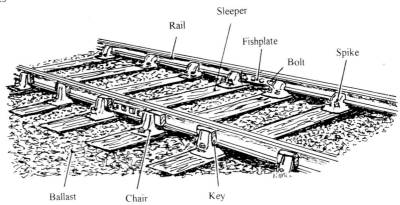

was not readily available in such large quantities until Gilchrist and Gilchrist-Thomas, of Middlesbrough, invented their phosphorus-removing furnace in 1878.

English Jurassic iron ores are notorious for their phosphorus content which makes steel brittle, then crack relatively easily. A classic example of the effects of these factors can be found in St Neots Museum where there is an analysis of the crash inspector's report into the St Neots rail crash of 1895.

The archivists at the National Railway Museum at York came up with no suggestions as to where such a line could have existed in the Kimbolton area, even for a short time. Except for one long shot of a guess. Remember the iron ore quarry at Raunds? This was the only standard gauge iron ore quarry rail track to be built in the last century in the East Midlands. When it was built it ran from Raunds Station to the quarry in the town, being just over a mile in length. Apparently it can still be seen in one or two places, mostly buried under decades of dust, soil and vegetation.

Fig 43 - Raunds Ironstone Railway map, 1879

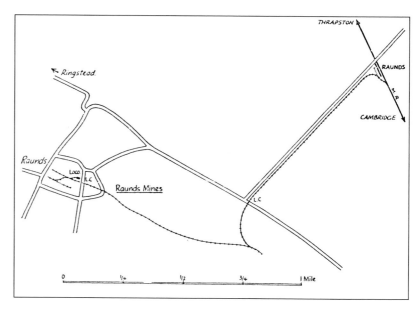

If one goes back to the comments about heavy goods unloading facilities possibly not being available at all the smaller stations in 1871, one could envisage the equipment being delivered to Kimbolton for railing to Raunds. There was a gap of just under eight years, however, between delivery at Kimbolton and the opening of the Raunds Ironstone Quarry, which makes this most unlikely. Does this mean that Mr. Golightly, the receiver of the railtrack equipment, was anticipating an eastward extension of the Thrapston ore deposits? Who was Mr. Golightly? Are any of his descendants still living in the Kimbolton area? These were questions buzzing through my mind.

In Appendix One an earlier reference to Mr Golightly can be found on September 16th 1866. On this day he received "two crossings" from Sheffield.

The Huntingdon Record Office could find no reference to Mr Golightly in the 1871 census so he may have been a railway agent brought into the town for a few months only to oversee a project. The following table lists the materials delivered to Kimbolton Station for Mr Golightly;-

The Railway Equipment Deliveries for Mr Golightly

Date From	No. Materials	Weight	Carter
Feb 1 Masboro'	300 Rails	61t 9c 3q	F. Waller X
Feb 2 Masboro'	228 Rails	46t 16c	T. Weggs
Feb 16 Derby	3750	Chairs	G. Millard X
	1060 Plates	48t 1c 3q	

Feb 22	Derby Bolts&Keys	2t 10c	
Mar 18	Derby 3000 Spikes	1t	S.Bunning
Mar 22	Grimsby 622 Sleepers	32t 15c	S.Bunning
Mar 23	Grimsby 1228 Sleepers	64t 15c	S.Bunning
Mar 28	Derby 6000 Spikes	2t	H. Smith
May 25	Thrapstone (10?) Some Rails	2t	S.Bunning
June 26	Thrapstone Fencing	2t	
July 27	Thrapstone Slag	5t 10c	W.Brunning
Aug 3	Thrapstone Slag	16t	W.Brunning
Aug 7	Thrapstone Slag	26t 10c	W.Brunning
Aug 21	Nottingham Set of Angles	2t	

X - may imply that the carter could not write.

Derby was the headquarters of the Midland Railway, and where the company's main engineering works and central offices were located. Masborough was a steel-making centre in Rotherham, southern Yorkshire and was on the Midland network. Grimsby, on the eastern end of the Manchester, Sheffield & Lincolnshire Railway, was a major port for the import of wooden railway sleepers from Scandinavia. The consignment of some rails" from Thrapston, suggests that the original orders for rails fell slightly short of Mr. Golightly's needs, and implies that the ironworks in Thrapston had a rolling mill capable of producing such an order.

Where could these materials have been destined? Catworth? There were plenty of traders in that village using the station, and many orders were destined for villages to the north of the present A14 trunk road. The terrain was on the level, but there is no evidence to be found either in old records, local folklore or old track bed foundations. The Covington brickworks? They were about one mile from the station, but there was a hill along the line of a potential route. The same limitation applied to Kimbolton.

The most likely use for these railway materials could be related to the fact that this cross-country single-track railway had only been open for just four years and it is possible that the line's goods facilities, including those at Kimbolton, were being expanded as the demand for them grew. This may have meant that additional sidings had to be built. As has been stated there were only 3.5 tons of coal delivered to the station in 1871 but this had increased dramatically to an annual 3,500 tons a couple of years later. This would have required more sidings.

Extra sidings may also have been built at Raunds, Grafham and Buckden. Kimbolton may well have been the concentration point from which work gangs drew on supplies. But where did Mr. Golightly fit into the picture? Was he a Midland Railway agent?

The most likely answer to all these questions was discovered through a search of the national census records. The Golightly name appears to be native to North East England, where over seven hundred references are recorded. Few appear to have left the area, but one was William Golightly, who was born in Frosterley, Weardale, Co. Durham, aged 56 in 1871. This person had become a Head Railway Superintendent in Leicester by 1881.

The 1891 census for Leicester shows that William Golightly, aged 76, had retired from his post as railway superintendent, and was living at number 5 Blyth Terrace, Upper Fox Street with his wife Mary, daughter Mary Rowell and her son Charles William . Further details from the census show that William senior's wife originated from Haydon Bridge, Co. Durham, daughter Mary was born in 1852 at Collingham, Lincolnshire, which is five miles north east of Newark on the Midland Railway line from Nottingham to Lincoln. Charles, aged 17 in the census, was born in Leicester in 1874.

Occasionally, it is interesting to explore the social side of a person's life. William Golightly was a divisional superintendent whose house was near to Leicester Station to the east of the main line. His residence was not particularly large; it was set back slightly from the pavement, and had a reasonably well-proportioned rear garden. All this reflected fairly on his status in the company. The whole street was cleared in stages, the last in 1970 when 5 Upper Fox Street was razed to the ground

William Golightly's will, published after his death in 1901, and now lodged at the Leicestershire Record Office, describes him as 'formerly superintendent of way & works of Midland Railway". All this suggests that he worked for the Midland Railway at Collingham during 1852 but was re-located to Leicester by 1866, possibly due to promotion. His retirement might have been precipitated when the post of divisionsal superintendent was abolished, to be replaced by inspectors

G. B. 58 **Midland Railway.**

Live Stock Receipt Note, No. 29

Date July 1879

From KIMBOLTON to St Pancras

Description No.	Kind	Quantity of Wagons	Rate per Wagon	Paid on	Paid £	s.	d.	To Pay £	s.	d.
16	Sheep	1						1	0	0

To be signed by the Owner or some person authorised to do so on his behalf.

Name of Consignee Millard

I have received the counterpart of this Ticket and agree to abide by the conditions expressed on the back hereof in consideration of the Company's charging me as above being less than they are by statute entitled to charge.

Witness ... The Owner or on the Owner's behalf.

Clerk to the Midland Railway Company.

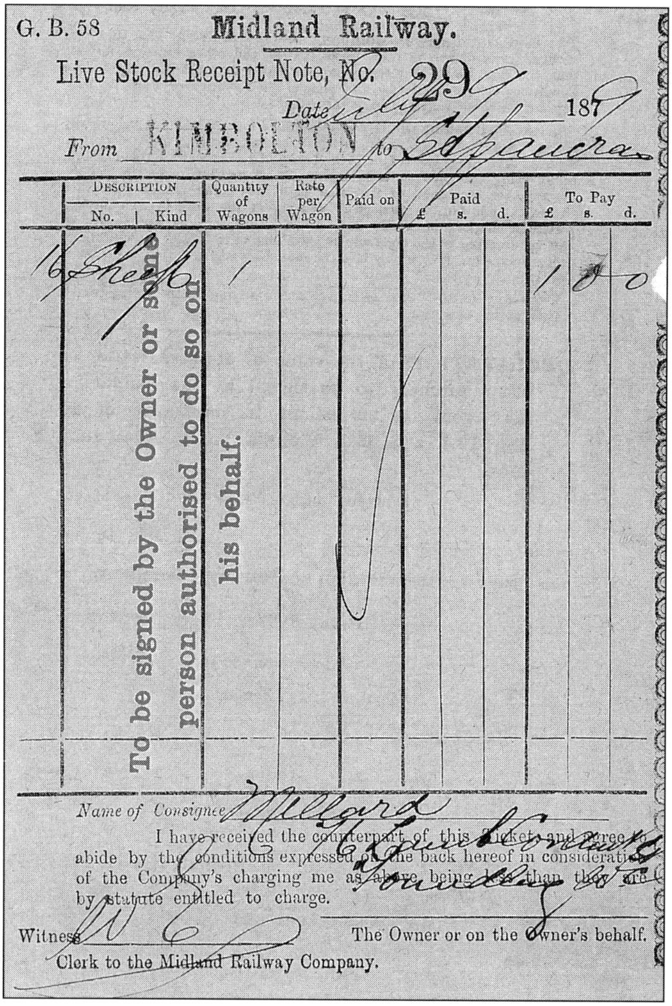

Fig 44 - Livestock Movement from Kimbolton in 1879

Another William Golightly, who was born in Hilton, Co. Durham, lived in Aston, Birmingham in 1881. He was a Head Railway Inspector! Were the two Williams related? His wife came from Nottingham and his daughter was born in (yes, you've guessed it) Leicester! He could well have been the son of the older William Golightly.

By now, you may well have formed an opinion that Mr Golightly could have laid extra sidings facilities at the stations along the Kimbolton line five years after the official opening. Being raised in Frosterley in 1815 he would already have been introduced to the exciting prospects for railway transport, for that village was located in Weardale and only three miles from the terminus for one of the world's earliest railways namely the 1829 Stanhope & Tyne Railway. More than half of this line was hauled by ropes and stationary steam engines. This youthful experience on his own doorstep must have given him a vision of future transport, and so enticed him into that profession.

Eight Years Later – Animal Movements in 1879-80

Eight years on from the 'Goods Delivery' book of 1871, a complete set of livestock forwarding bills, representing a full year's movements, gives the reader a detailed insight into the nature of the pastoral farming industry in the Kimbolton area.

The local farming industry relied upon markets for its produce, and it was no surprise there was a considerable export of cattle (identified as 'beast' on the bills), sheep and pigs to the towns and cities. The occasional bull or horse also passed through the station yard for Huntingdon or Kettering.

The despatch of cattle, sheep and pigs showed a definite autumn peak followed by a summer lull when animals would have been taking advantage of lush pastures. Sheep and lambs were sold after summer fattening and their movements show a dramatic increase from August to November, possibly in preparation for Christmas, followed by a sharp decrease in mid-December. Refrigeration was not used until much later so all animals had to be transported live to areas where demand was greatest, and then eaten quickly after being slaughtered and salted.

Fig 45 - Kimbolton Station and Goods Yard in 1902

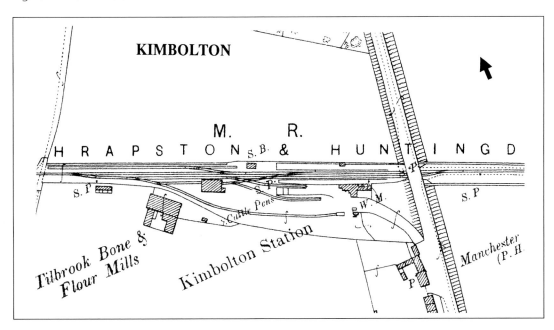

Kimbolton's goods yard had specially constructed sidings with animal pens, and this loading bay handled over one hundred and fifty animal trucks a year by this time. The total numbers of animals despatched in 1880 are shown in the table below. It is obvious that pastoral farming was dominated by cattle and sheep rearing. There were 31 cattle, 32 sheep and 10 pig shipments during the year. The columns show both the number of shipments followed by the number of animals despatched to each of the market towns.

	Cattle nos.	Sheep Nos.	Pig Nos.	Total Animals
St. Ives	15 - 25	19 - 998	3 - 83	1337
Cambridge	9 - 126	0	0	126
Northampton	0	1 - 20	3 - 24	44
Kettering	1 - 21	1 - 19	0	40
Thrapston	3 - 19	3 - 54	4 - 24	97
Birmingham	2 - 6	0	0	6
Wellingborough	0	1 - 13	0	13
St. Pancras	0	6 - 114	0	114
Rushden	1 - 1	0	0	1
Cranford	0	1 - 70(lambs)	0	70
Totals	31 - 429	32 - 1288	10 - 131	1848

Fig 46 - Kimbolton Station's monthly outflow of livestock in 1880

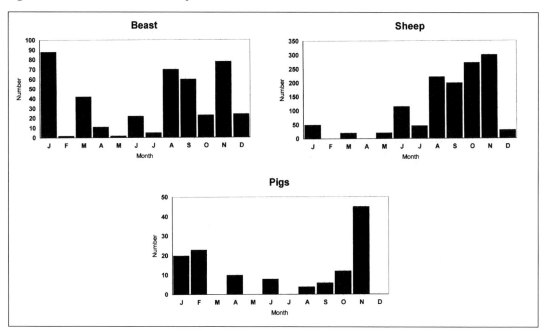

The most important livestock market in the area was at St. Ives. The Midland Railway's metals ended in Huntingdon at the East Station, which was adjacent to the present-day mainline station. The company's running powers over the Great Northern & Great Eastern Joint Railway line to St. Ives allowed a smooth operation of the business.

St. Ives was an interesting junction station with lines radiating out to March, Ramsey (via Somersham) and Ely, as well as to Huntingdon and Cambridge. This made the location a natural hub for animals to be brought for auction and redistribution. The cattle pens were on the west side of the March line and just outside the station's main entrance. The detailed large-scale map (fig 47) shows there were ten large and twelve small pens separated from a huge series of open stalls by two sidings. Such was the size and importance of the market at the time.

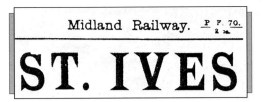

Fig 47 - St Ives Station and Cattle Market in 1887

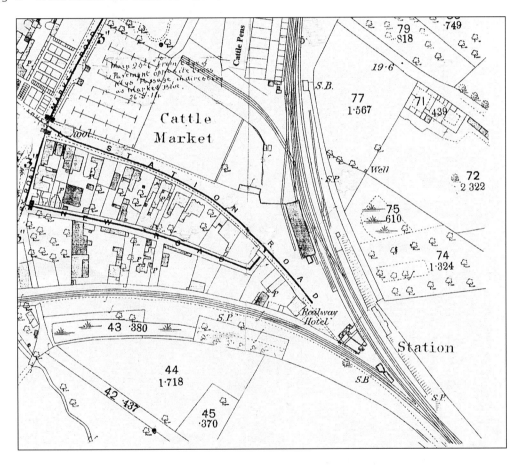

How was the farm animal dealt with on its journey from farm to final destination? A classical procedure was likely to involve at least two 'middle-men', or agents. A farmer would sell his animals to a local agent, like Thomas H Spicer, also a baker, of 24, East Street, Kimbolton. He had a contact agent in London, a Mr. Millard, of 76, Lamb's Conduit St., Russell Square, London with whom he would strike a deal. The farmer would take his sheep to Kimbolton Station where they would be loaded for transport to St. Pancras via Kettering goods yard, with final transfer to a specified London butcher.

There were several agents in St. Ives who bought local animals for shipment to their final destinations. A surprising trade was discovered in cattle sales to Norwich, even though that area had its own beef-rearing marshes such as Halvergate. Mr. Hall, of Bythorn was a regular user of Kimbolton Station for shipping his farm animals to distant markets. On August 26th 1880 he drove "fifteen beast" to the station for shipment to Mr. Stroyan of Norwich.

When the animals were loaded on to a wagon its registered number would have been added to each way-bill for easy checking. According to the paperwork Mr. Hall made sure the costs of carriage were paid by Mr. Stroyan.

Fig 48 - Midland Railway wagon registration plate

Two other examples of Mr. Hall's trade were found. On August 15, 1879 he sent a hundred lambs to John Hall (relative?) of Ashwell, via Cambridge, presumably for fattening. The railway used two trucks for this contract, numbered 6094 and 23052. On July 31, 1880 Mr. Hall sent "4 fat heifers" to Mr. Blake of St. Ives.

The names of two further 1879 dealers in St. Ives were Mr. Radford, who bought twenty pigs from Wornditch, adjacent to Kimbolton, and Mr. Northropp, cattle dealer, who received a truck with eight beast from Edwin Throssell and three from Mr. Brightman of Great Staughton. In addition Thomas Browning, of Keysoe, sent seventy lambs to St. Ives for forwarding to Mr. Smith of Caxton. This required ten miles of droving by road to satisfy the order.

Branding, in some form, must have been used to distinguish ownership, for a single wagon was likely to contain animals from more than one farm An 1868 consignment note (fig 49) for Mr Chapman's sheep confirms the existence of an identification marking system.

Fig 49 - Animal Marking for Identification

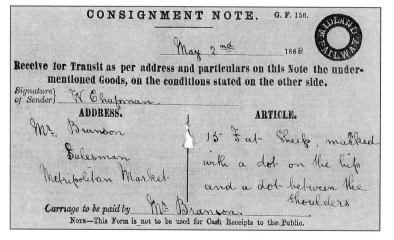

Finally, this section would not be complete without mentioning that Tilbrook's wholesaler and agent TH Smith's had his 'finger in the pie'. In one 1879 order he asked the station agent to send "the Half Truck (of) Horses To Hitchin Station carriage forward for Mr. Thos. Priest of Ickleford near Hitchin".

Mushy Peas?

The handling of arable produce is well documented. The paperwork shows that the district produced a large amount of cereals, peas and beans for large industrial centres, and the method of marketing was similar to that for animals. The usual route was from farm to station to final destination with the paperwork and money being handled by agents at each end.

Simple? Well, not quite. There are two examples that are worthy of mention. The first was for 14 quarters (180 kgs) of peas in May 1882, and was a little more complicated than usual. Thomas Spicer bought them off a farmer and sold them to Mr D Gibson of Boston in Lincolnshire who then arranged a further contract with an agent at Waterloo Station, North Liverpool Docks on the London & North Western Railway.

More peas were sold by Mr Pashler, via Thomas Spicer, to Mr. Woodhead of Leeds. This was a much simpler sale, the order being transported throughout by the Midland Railway.

Blott on the Landscape

In January 1882, Mr Lewin of Brington, sent a bulk sample of barley to merchant William Blott & Co. of Wellingborough. Blott sent the barley on to Stafford & Shutes of Station Road, Nottingham, possibly for use in the city's brewery industry, now sadly extinct. In rejecting the sample Stafford & Shutes said the barley was of unacceptable quality, presumably for malting, so it was transferred back to Wellingborough.

Fig 50 - William Blott, corn merchants, Wellingborough letterhead 1882

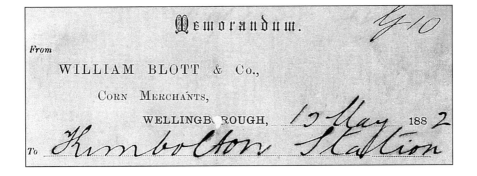

The Two Tommies

Thomas Smith and Thomas Spicer were two major local traders whose activities were influenced by the arrival of the railway.

Thomas Spicer lived from 1847 to 1924, making him 24 years old in 1871. He was regarded as being a town baker who lived and worked at 24, East Street, Kimbolton. He supported the work of the town by being a member of the Vestry, a type of local council in the Nineteenth Century. What this study has discovered is that he was not only a baker but also a middle-man that local farmers turned to for help when they wanted to buy and sell produce. He took advantage of the railway's telegraph system, for speed and efficiency, and was prepared to do the paperwork for transactions over animal and crop sales. Not everyone could read and write in those days, let alone spell.

Fig 51 - Mr & Mrs Thomas Spicer outside their bakery in Kimbolton

Fig 52 - Thomas Spicer's
headed notepaper

According to a number of Consignment Notes and the 'Goods Delivery' book from 1868 there was a Mr H Smith living in Great Catworth, one mile due north of the station, who traded in a wide range of goods such as cloth, food, tea, meat and domestic equipment, and sold sheep on to other agents on behalf of local farmers. His chief traded commodity was fat sheep.

There was no reference to H Smith in the 'Goods Delivery' book for 1871, but a Mr TH Smith, aged eighteen, appeared frequently. It was obvious he was running a very large business buying and selling almost every commodity under the sun, including horses, although he tended to leave building and engineering materials to the experts. Was H Smith the father of TH Smith? If so, did the former pass the reins of the business over to his son between 1868 and 1871? It was too enormous a business for someone to have built up in a mere two years unless it had been bought, or inherited, from an already well-established concern. Thomas H Smith operated his business from Tilbrook, one mile down the hill and south of the station.

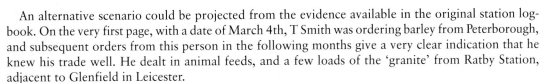
An alternative scenario could be projected from the evidence available in the original station log-book. On the very first page, with a date of March 4th, T Smith was ordering barley from Peterborough, and subsequent orders from this person in the following months give a very clear indication that he knew his trade well. He dealt in animal feeds, and a few loads of the 'granite' from Ratby Station, adjacent to Glenfield in Leicester.

Not all that remarkable, I hear you say, but shuffle these facts around in your mind and see if they lead you to similar conclusions to my own. There was a T Smith trading in 1866 in a small way from an unnamed settlement. In 1868 H Smith was dealing from Great Catworth, as described two para-graphs earlier, and finally TH Smith was recorded in late 1870 from Tilbrook.

Were all these three people one and the same or was the father/son relationship the more likely explanation? If the former, this is a story of a remarkable young man who started trading at the tender age of thirteen! If you can accept the enormity of that concept, it begs the question as to where he acquired such an education to equip him with the skills for this successful launch into a professional career.

The 1800 Inclosure map of Tilbrook (fig 54) shows that there must have been a well-endowed school in the village because it owned six parcels of land and rented two more, all within that settle-ment. The preceding comment is all hypothetical, of course, but local detectives will be much better placed than me to explore the census archives for definitive information on this family's mid-Nine-teenth Century's history.

Whatever the final outcome, analysis of the 1871 'Goods Delivery' shows that Thomas Smith was the man people turned to for supplies for anything to do with food, farms and daily living. He could write, spell and obviously had great reserves of energy, enthusiasm, initiative and entrepreneurial skill.

A comparison of the 1868 and 1871 'Goods Delivery' books shows a number of differences. In the earlier register there is no mention of animal feedstuffs and fertilizer, yet three years later, probably due to TH Smith's energetic dealings, the later register is dominated by a large range of exotic animal feeds described in earlier sections. This may pin-point the date when such changes occurred in the agricultural activities of the Kimbolton area, and the gentleman responsible for this metamorphosis.

Fig 53 - T H Smith Instruction Note

The question of where Thomas Smith operated from in Tilbrook, proved rather difficult to an-swer. 130 years on one needs to look for buildings that were capable of supporting such a large operation, and many changes might have occurred in the intervening period. With such volumes of goods involved he must have used a large warehouse or barn complex.

> TILBROOK, *19" May.* 188*2*
>
> The Station Master, *Kimbolton*
>
> Sir,
>
> Please receive from Mr. *T. Blackwell of Wornditch* about *30 Qrs. Beans 19" nett in Rail* Sacks,
> and *Transfer* the same to *at your Station*
> To Mr. *C.J.K Woolstone*
> *of Wellingboro*
>
> *Fill up annexed Form and return to me.*
>
> *Yours truly,*
>
> T. H. SMITH.

Fortunately, there is one such set of old shiplap barns in the village, down Station Road, which might have fitted the bill. Thomas Smith, at the age of 28, lived in Back Street, in the 47th Tilbrook house tackled by the 1881 census. Apparently, houses in the village were not numbered in those days. The three main streets in Tilbrook in 1881 appear to have been Back Street, Front Street and Higham Road. In the 1891 census Back Street had been renamed North Street, and by 1910 only two side roads could be identified, namely Cheap Street and Station Road. It appears that North Street was renamed, for a second time, to become Station Road.

Fig 54 - Inclosure Map for Tilbrook - 1800

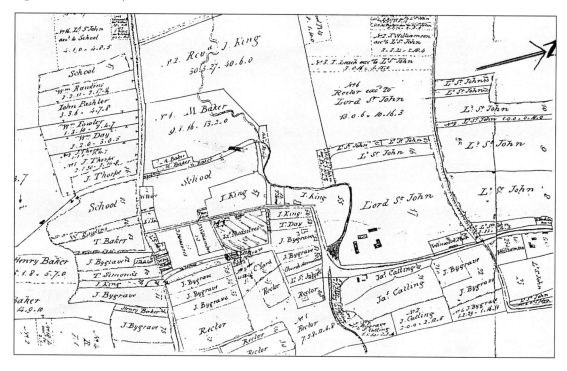

Fig 55 - Tilbrook Census 1881 with T H Smith's Details

Page 8] The undermentioned Houses are situate within the Boundaries of the Parish of Tilbrook

Civil Parish [or Township] of	City or Municipal Borough of	Municipal Ward of	Parliamentary Borough of	Town or Village or Hamlet of	Urban Sanitary District of	Rural Sanitary District of	Ecclesiastical Parish or District of
Tilbrook				Tilbrook		St. Neots	Tilbrook

No. of Schedule	ROAD, STREET, &c., and No. or NAME of HOUSE	HOUSES Inhabited	HOUSES Uninhabited (U.), or Building (B.)	NAME and Surname of each Person	RELATION to Head of Family	CONDITION as to Marriage	AGE last Birthday of Males	AGE last Birthday of Females	Rank, Profession, or OCCUPATION	WHERE BORN	If (1) Deaf-and-Dumb (2) Blind (3) Imbecile or Idiot (4) Lunatic
46	Back Street	1		Henry Furnall	Head	Mar	31		Groom	Huntingdon Sh. Bythorn	
				Eliza do	Wife	do		33		Bedford Sh. Eaton Socon	
				Walter G. do	Son		8		Scholar	Huntingdon Sh. Bythorn	
				Ernest H. do	do		6		do	do do	
				Kate do	Daur			3		do Catworth	
				Ellen do	do			1		do do	
47	do	1		Thomas H. Smith	Head	Mar	28		Corn Merchant	Bedford Sh. Tilbrook	
				Sarah C. do	Wife	do		33	Corn Merchant's Wife	Huntingdon Sh. Brington	
				Edith C. do	Daur			4		Bedford Sh. Tilbrook	
				Thomas H. L. do	Son		2			do do	
				Sidney do	Son		1			do do	
				Mary Roddis	Servant	Unm		23	General Serv	do Pertenhall	
				Lucy Coles	do	Unm		40	Nursemaid	Huntingdon Sh. Keyston	
48	do	1		Thomas Hewitt	Head	Mar	53		Ag Labr	Bedford Sh. Tilbrook	
				Alice do	Wife	do		52		Huntingdon Sh. Hamerton	

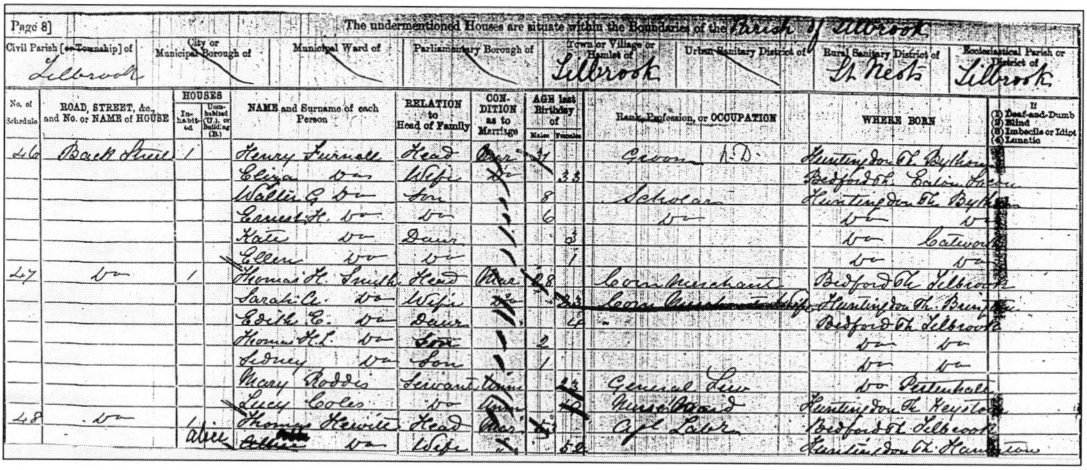

The origin of the shiplap barns was researched. The land was owned by James Measures on the 1800 inclosure map, and a beam in one of the barns still bears the name "Measures" carved on it with a date in the 1880's. This suggests continuous ownership by the Measures family through the Smith period.

According to the 1881 census Thomas Smith was married, with three children at school, and had two servants. This suggested a degree of affluence, but by 1910, when an Inland Revenue Land Values Duty map was compiled, there was no sign of the family in the village. Either Thomas had died or moved away to a more substantial house in another settlement.

It was discovered that the Measures family farmed from Tilbrook Grange (Fig 8) in the Nineteenth Century. The Grange was adjacent to the station and is now inhabited by the Hunter family. The Measures owned three small parcels of land in Tilbrook, including the farm with the shiplap barns.

The most feasible explanation, if there is one, is that Thomas Smith, aged 18 in 1871, either inherited the business from his father in Great Catworth or transferred his rapidly expanding business from Catworth to larger premises in Tilbrook. He had visionary ideas for expansion into goods being made available by the railway, and rented the farm from the Measures' estate to cope with these increased volumes of goods.

By 1879 Thomas Smith's commercial operation was so considerable that it warranted separate record books for delivered goods. The second book in this series has survived, and contains records for about three and a half years. A full analysis has not been possible in the time available, but a brief study has identified trends which were different from those at the start of the decade:-

1. Thomas Smith's activities had become much more restricted to farm products.
2. Animal feeds had shrunk back to a more basic list, shedding the more exotic ones of ten years earlier. Gone were locust beans and palm nut meal.
3. More seriously, when numbers of orders were counted, there was a steady decline between March 1879 and September 1882, ending with a dramatic fall in the last month, as seen here in fig 56.

Fig 56 - TH Smith's monthly orders' volume via Kimbolton Station 1879-82

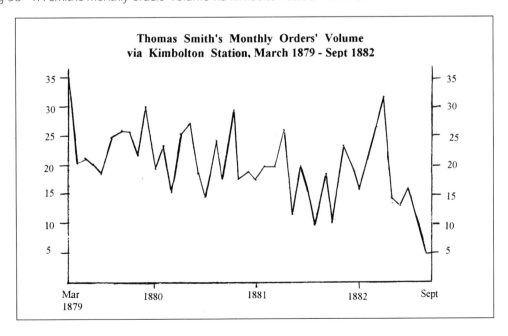

If you cast your eyes back to the 1902 Kimbolton Station map (fig 45), you will note the "Tilbrook Bone & Flour Mills" adjacent to the goods yard. Why was the name "Tilbrook" used? Did Thomas Smith relocate his commercial operation and expand into processing in addition to dealing in animal feeds? The name begs the question as to why the mills were not named after the station, unless there was a connection with the owner. Unfortunately again, no records of the mills are held at the Huntingdon Record Office.

There may have been greater competition from such people as Thomas Spicer, or there may have been ill health dogging Smith. Indeed, an analysis of another 1881 'Delivery Book', shows that Thomas Spicer was much more important than ten years earlier.

Taking aside Thomas Smith's order book, Spicer was responsible for generating fifty four per cent of the remaining deliveries at the station. There were, in addition, two other smaller competitors based in Tilbrook. By this date the station had lost all its 1871 users from the villages to the north of the current A14 trunk road.

Fig 57 - Hinterland of Kimbolton Station in 1881

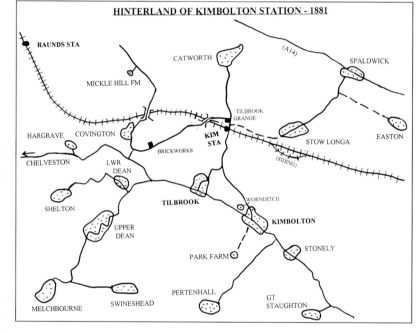

HINTERLAND OF KIMBOLTON STATION - 1881

The Daily Working of the Railway

This last section will deal with two aspects of the daily operations of the station, namely the telegraph and timetables. The latter include the signal-box register.

Passenger and Goods Timetables

The 1870-1 signal-box register gives us an insight into the daily operation of the line. Selected weekly movements and timings can be found in Appendix 4.

These consist of a week in March 1870 and one in August of the same year. It can be seen that there was no variation in passenger services between winter and summer, there being four trains in each direction on weekdays and none on Sundays.

You will also note that the register contains details of both booked and actual "arrival" and "departure" times of trains. These meticulous records show that two of the passenger trains were timed to cross at Kimbolton. The analysis of the register confirmed the comments in John Rhodes book that the line had a reputation for poor timekeeping, and affected about 10 per cent of the trains.

Goods traffic had a well-established timetable with three trains a day in each direction, all after mid-day. In reality the punctuality of the goods service was variable. This would have led to some hectic activity in the goods yard on the occasions when the trains were up to three and a half hours late, and especially if they conveyed livestock and fresh food products.

Weekend goods traffic ran in both the summer and winter. In March 1870 the Saturday service was the same as that on Mondays to Fridays and there was one goods train on Sundays for Kettering just after mid-day. In the summer there was one train in each direction on Saturdays and Sundays with an extra "Down" service just after 7 pm on Sundays. So, no time for church attendance at Kimbolton or Great Catworth for the goods agent!

There were quite a lot of "Special Trains" recorded in the register. Between January 1870 and early February 1871 highlighted these facts. First, there were 94 "Specials" and they operated on the following days of the week:-

Monday	Tuesday	Wednesday	Thursday	Friday	Saturday	Sunday
21	11	3	3	21	27	8
(Oct/Nov)	(Nov/Dec)					

The "Specials" were seasonal in character as shown below. The pattern suggests a stocking-up of goods for winter in October and November:-

Month	Jan	Feb	Mar	Apr	May	Jun	Jul	Aug	Sep	Oct	Nov	Dec
	2	3	3	3	9	4	5	1	11	29	16	8

Fourteen of the "Specials" were identified as being for cattle and just called intermediately at Kimbolton. In addition there were seven trains which arrived from Kettering, picked up unidentified goods at Kimbolton and then returned to Kettering.

There were four, possibly excursion, "Passenger Specials" in May, June and July all of which ran on Tuesdays. Three steamed on in the direction of Huntingdon while the fourth travelled on towards Kettering.

The (Electric) Telegraph

This was a form of communication between stations, signal-boxes and commercial offices, which used electrical impulses along copper wires erected alongside rail tracks. The impulses conveyed messages by Morse code.

According to the hugely informative "Oxford Companion to British Railway History", experiments in this form of message started in the late 1820's using electricity and magnetism. An experimental installation on the line from London to Camden (on the newly opened London & Birmingham Railway), in 1838, was successful but the company turned it down. The Great Western Railway was more impressed and used it out of Paddington in 1839. Its reputation, as a means of communication, was proved when a murderer, escaping from Slough to Paddington by train in 1845, was caught after his details were forwarded by telegraph.

This success led to the creation of a number of telegraph companies which quickly set up a national network alongside canals and railways. The network was nationalised as early as 1869 and was operated by the Post Office. The railway companies were allowed to continue to operate their own system and the last stretch of telegraph was in use, in Sussex, as late as 1972!

The cost of installation of the telegraph from Kettering to Kimbolton was probably in the region of £800. This is how much a similar length of telegraph line cost in the same decade between Grantham and Nottingham.

Fig 58 - Post Office Telegraph Note 1881

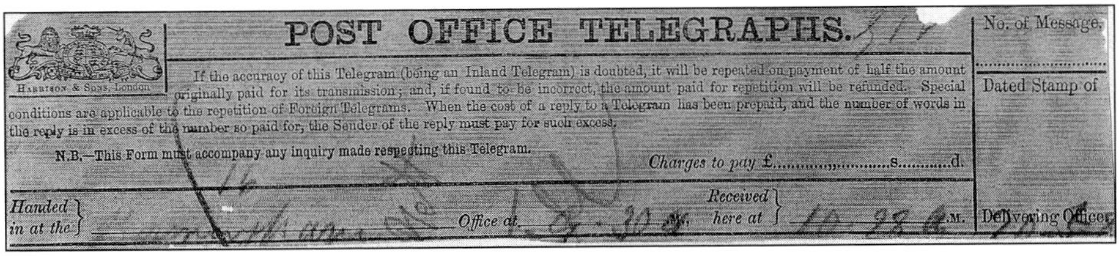
POST OFFICE TELEGRAPHS.

No. of Message.

Harrison & Sons, London

If the accuracy of this Telegram (being an Inland Telegram) is doubted, it will be repeated on payment of half the amount originally paid for its transmission; and, if found to be incorrect, the amount paid for repetition will be refunded. Special conditions are applicable to the repetition of Foreign Telegrams. When the cost of a reply to a Telegram has been prepaid, and the number of words in the reply is in excess of the number so paid for, the Sender of the reply must pay for such excess.

Dated Stamp of

N.B.—This Form must accompany any inquiry made respecting this Telegram.

Charges to pay £............s..........d.

Handed in at the .... *Office at* .... M. *Received here at* .... M.

Delivering Officer

One interesting booklet, found at Kimbolton Station, gave details of the costs of telegraph messages to North America and the West Indies via the Transatlantic Cable in 1871. This could well have been the cable laid down by the "SS Great Eastern" of Isambard Kingdom Brunel fame. The quoted costs per word for telegraphing over such distances were enormous, but it must have been worth it because many orders were transmitted in those days from ports like Liverpool for cotton, wheat and sugar.

One interesting section stated that all messages bound for Cuba must be in Spanish or English and not in secret code. The Spanish were worried about independence movements on the island at the time.

Fig 59 - Kimbolton linked to North America via the telegraph in 1871

TARIFF

FOR THE

TRANSMISSION OF MESSAGES

BY THE

Anglo-American & French Atlantic Cables

TO THE

UNITED STATES OF AMERICA,

&c., &c., &c.,

ISSUED

JULY 1st, 1871.

————◆————

Offices of both Companies :—

26, OLD BROAD STREET, LONDON, E.C.

The Signal-box

As one can see from the extract below, the details for each train's arrival were recorded without fail. These included the engine's number (see Appendix 4), times of arrival and departure and the name of the guard.

Guards operating on the Line in 1869-70 were:-

Simmons Whitby R. Holmes

Hallam Towers Williamson

Jarratt Hagley Simms

Woods Keatch
(on "Special Trains" only)

This register was completed by two signalmen named Bolton and Webster, who seemed to be sharing the same job each day. Occasionally James Ibbs would act as relief signalman. Until November 1870 all trains arriving at Kimbolton were identified as "passenger" or "goods", but the practice was replaced thereafter by counting the number of "vehicles" on the train.

Fig 60 - Extract from Signal-box Log Book 1869 -'Up' line from Kettering

Up

Date	Due	Arrival	Dept	Descrip	No of Engine	
July 14	8-26	8-27	8-36	Pass	42	Wills
"	11-48	11-50	11-51	"	44	T Simmons
"	3-33	3-40	3-42	"	42	T Whitby
"	4-48	5-5	5-15	Goods	709	J. Williamson

[illegible]

July 14						
"	8..1	8..0	8..4	Pass	44	T. Simmons
15th	12..30	12..47	1..15	Goods	491	R. Holmes
"	5..8	5..30	5..37	"	493	T. Hallam

Wm Bolton

July 15	8-26	8-32	8-35	Pass	49	T Whitby
"	11-45	11-49	11-51	"	44	T Simmons
"	Balast	11-0	11-1	Balast	322	Williamson
"	3-32	3-56	3-59	Pass	49	~~T Simmons~~ T Whitby
"	4-48	4-53	5-10	Goods	713	G Farrall

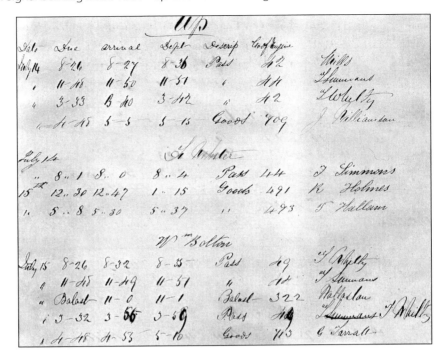

Fig 61 - Extract from Signal-box Log Book 1869 - 'Down' line from Huntingdon

Down

Date	Due	Arrvl	Dept	Report	No of Eng	No of Vehs	Name of Guard
Decm 10	12-31	12-31	12-26		715		G. Farrall
" "	8.27	8.32	8.34		46	5	T Simmons
" "	12.38	12.40	12.42	12.19	41	4	T Whitby
" "	1/50	2.25	2.45		628		J. Williamson
" "	3.34	3.35	3.53		46	4	T Simmons
" "	7-19	7-48	7-50	7-23	41	5	T. Whitby
" "	7-50	8-15	8-35		323		A. Gapp
" "	12-36	1-15	1-30		245		T. Hallam
" 12	8.27	8.34	8-36	8.10	46	5	T Simmons
" "	12-38	12.41	12.42	12.18	41	4	T Whitby
" "	1.50	2.10	2.25		628		J. Williamson
" "	3.34	3.45	3-47		46	11	T Simmons
" "	7-19	7-17	7-19		41	5	T. Whitby
" "	7-50	8-2	8-7		323		G. Hagly
	12-36	12.45	1-1		715		T. Hallam

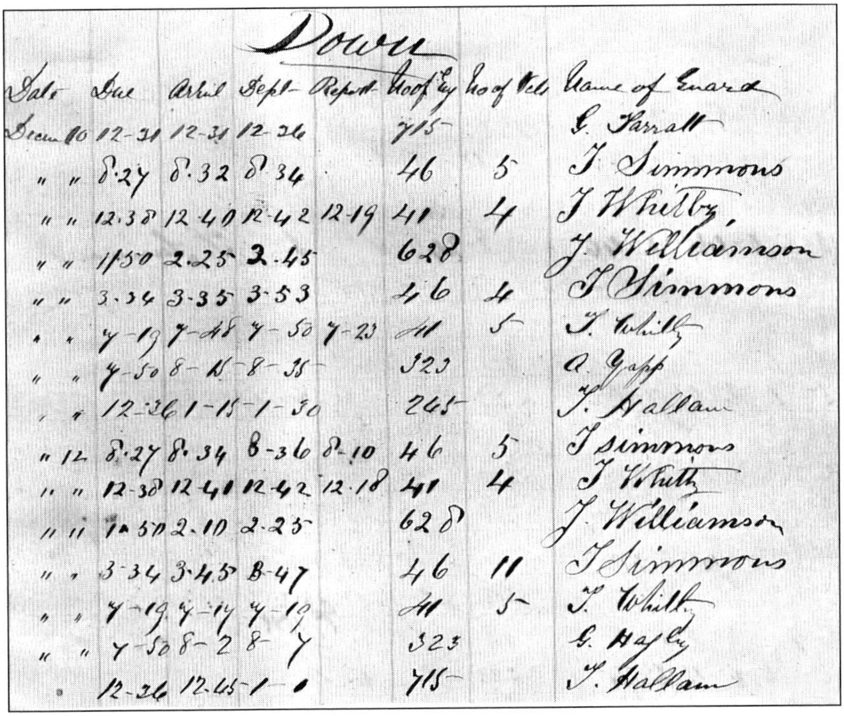

The Engines that Served Kimbolton, 1866-69

When the line opened in 1866 the first engines allocated to the everyday working of the scheduled services were probably some of those identified in the signal-box register of 1869-70 (Appendix 3). They were nearly twenty years old and not far from the end of their serviceable lives.

The engines were designed by the first Midland Railway locomotive superintendent, Matthew Kirtley, who was born at Tanfield, Co. Durham. Tanfield was the home to one of the world's first railways. If you cast your mind back to the discussion on the "Ghost Train" this was also William Golightly's home county, and these two men, who became so influential in the early days of the Midland Railway, probably acquired their inspiration and vision for the future from these early origins.

Kirtley was reputed to be the first engine driver, in his earlier career, to steam an engine into Euston on the station's opening day in 1838. He went on to be appointed the first Locomotive Superintendent of the Midland Railway by George Hudson, upon the formation of the company in 1844. The other applicant for the job was Matthew's brother Thomas!

The engines in the new company had, quite naturally, originated from the three amalgamating companies. They were unreliable and susceptible to frequent costly delays. Kirtley set about designing "rugged good steamers", according to the late Bertram Baxter in his book "British Locomotive Catalogue, Vol. 3A 1825-1923".

The wheel arrangement of a steam engine is described in three groups of axles, namely the front bogie wheels (two per axle) followed by the driving wheels and finally the rear bogies. The biggest engines, in the Twentieth Century, were designed occasionally with four or more groups of axles.

Some of the first engines to work through Kimbolton started life as 2-2-2 models. They were some of the very first designed by Kirtley and had driving wheel diameters of 5'6" (1.66m). The engines were built by Sharp Bros. of Manchester in 1847-8, and had no cabs, so winter time meant a cold uncomfortable job for the footplate crew. The signal-box register of 1870 shows that these engines were used for hauling the passenger trains which were normally composed of four or five coaches.

Fig 62 - Sharp Bros. Passenger Engine in 1852

The engines were rebuilt between 1859-61 to provide four driving wheels (2-4-0) and more pulling power. This is probably why they were selected for this switch-back route with its heavy demands on strength. These five engines were withdrawn between 1872 and 1875 and broken up.

Another class of engine that worked over the line was the 240 Class 0-6-0, built by R & W Hawthorn, of Newcastle-upon-Tyne, in 1851. This class of engine was Kirtley's first standard design and six were noted in the register in 1870.

Fig 63 - R & W Hawthorn's 0-6-0 Goods Engine 1851

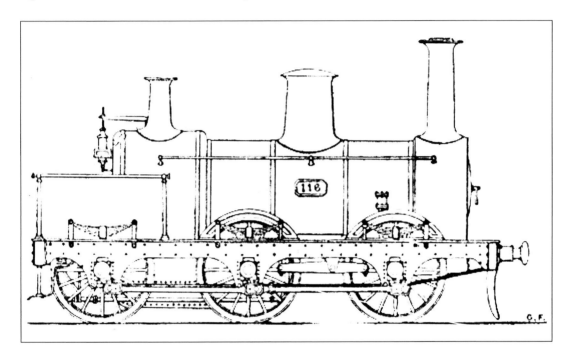

The first members of the 480 Class 0-6-0 of Standard Goods engines were built by Robert Stephenson of Darlington in 1863. Five of these sturdy 36 tonners were allocated to the line and remained in service until the early 1930's, a life of nearly seventy years!

The "Special Train" that steamed up and down the line quite frequently was No. 323 with Mr Keatch as the guard. This engine was also of the 480 Class built in 1865 at the Midland Railway's Workshops in Derby. These central engineering shops could not satisfy the demand at the time for this type of engine, hence the reason for them being constructed by private builders such as Stephenson and Sharp.

The 480 Class was very popular because nearly 250 of these engines were built between 1863 and 1869. Six more of the later 1868 models were supplied by Sharp, Stewart & Co. of Manchester and again lasted in service until 1930.

Fig 64 - 1857 0-6-0 Goods Engine Type Serving Kimbolton in 1870

Fig 65 - 0-6-0 Goods Engine Introduced in 1868 which served Kimbolton

Christmas presents came early to the footplate crews in 1869. A brand new class of 0-6-0 goods engine was introduced in that year and was called the 700 Class. Six made their way to this line. They were built by Dubs & Co. and Neilson & Co., both of Glasgow. Again these sturdy workhorses lasted until 1930, a testimony to Kirtley's qualities as a designer.

So, no exciting revelations about sparkling famous express engines roaring through Kimbolton in the dead of night. This is a story about a railway line which opened up a rural area while, at the same time, providing the Midland Railway with access from the South Midlands to Suffolk and Essex. It shows how a local community took advantage of the arrival of the railway and how it triggered off an enormous social and commercial revolution that lasted for eighty years until the piston engine nailed the coffin lid on this form of rural transport after the end of car rationing in 1954.

Competition from the East

The Midland Railway did not have all the trade to itself in Kimbolton! On March 24th, 1911 it was announced in a St Neots newspaper, that the Great Northern Railway was to open an agency at the Sun Inn, Kimbolton, where goods and parcels could be left for dispatch to all parts of the country. An omnibus was to leave Kimbolton for St Neots Station on Mondays, Wednesdays and Fridays with calls at Stonely, Great Staughton and Hail Weston for passengers and parcels.

The omnibus was timed to connect with the 1.42 pm train for London, and with the 1.36 pm Restaurant Car down train for Nottingham, Manchester, Liverpool and the chief towns in the north of England. Through carriages were attached to the latter train for Sheffield, Lincoln and Doncaster. How much damage this new service did to Kimbolton Station's trade is not known.

A Final Word

The last passenger train left Kimbolton Station on June 15th 1959 leaving the station open for goods only. Both services were withdrawn beyond Kimbolton to Huntingdon thus leaving the former a terminus until October 28th 1963 when the goods yard closed its doors for the last time.

Fig 66 - Two Tickets from the last Decade of Kimbolton Station's Existence

This sorry state of affairs left the station waiting for the track removal gang to arrive shortly afterwards. The photograph below was taken from the Catworth Road Bridge looking west towards Kettering on the 25th June 1967, showing how quickly nature reclaims its own territory with grass, weeds and blackberry bushes.

It has been a fascinating task unearthing this aspect of history from two centuries ago, but I feel I have only scratched at the surface of some of the topics. Who were these families? How many descendants still live in the same villages and are they still involved in the same careers? Where are the setts today?

Many people have helped enormously with this research. I would like to thank the following individuals and organisations for their expertise, support and willingness to provide me with relevant material and do tasks for me:-

John & Jean Stratford (Kimbolton Society), John Howlett, Charles Paull, Gavin Hunter of Kimbolton Station House, Roy Burrows (Sheffield Railwayana Auctions), Glynn Waite (Chairman, Midland

Fig 67 - Abandoned Kimbolton Station and Goods Yard in 1967

Railway Society), Allan Sibley (Great Northern Railway Society), Keith Osborne, Carol and Brian Stevens, S.E.C. Henson, Linda Reid, Barry Mills (researcher), Cambridge Collection, Huntingdon Record Office, Bedford Record Office, Northampton Record Office, Leics. Record Office, National Railway Museum (York), Christopher Awdry, Allan Mott, Peter Moyse (photographer), Ordnance Survey, British Geological Survey, Lafarge Redland, Derek Young, Simon Everard, Bob Gearey, Trevor Rushton, Peter Hall (LNER Study Group), Dr Mike Sharman, Dr John Gough, Richard Casserley and not least, my wife Dorothy, for all the physical tasks necessary for completion.

I am greatly indebted to Glynn Waite for his willingness to support me with his expertise in this small venture. He did not shirk from the responsibility to be honest and frank with me on many occasions when the need arose!

I would like to record the fact that it was Granville Rudd, the archaeologist and teacher at Long-sands College, St Neots, Cambridgeshire, who sowed the seeds of this idea fifteen years ago. His memory inspired me to 'have a go' when time became available.

Finally, I would like it to be known that I am an enthusiast, and not a technical expert, in all things mechanical that hiss. I have discovered that you can be driven to the point of distraction attempting to unearth the last possible accurate detail. That was not the purpose of this book. It was designed to give an insight into the influence that the arrival of the railway had on a rural area in mid-Victorian times, opening up new avenues for entrepreneurs in much the same way as the internet is changing our lives today - the latter system running parallel to a resurgence in railway communications, despite the Hatfield crash hiccough and the dithering of politicians.

BIBLIOGRAPHY

Canals of the East Midlands - Charles Hadfield

Branch Lines around Huntingdon - A Mott & C Awdry

Oxford Companion to British Railway History

Kettering to Huntingdon - John Rhodes

British Locomotive Catalogue, Vol 3A 1825-1923

Ellis & Everard Centenary 1848-1948

The Midland Railway : A Chronology - John Gough

Institute of Civil Engineering Proceedings, May 1892

London Illustrated Weekly News 1866

APPENDIX

Appendix One

Daily Incidents During the Early Months after the Station's Opening in 1866.
(A small sample only to illustrate incidents in the book.)

Date

21.2	Goods opening. Cart and machine arrived.
21.2	Guard Portans wages.
21.2	First invoice sent from station - for coal order from Pinxton, Derbyshire.
24.2	Leicester to Huntingdon train - arrived at 11.25am.
26.2	Leicester to Huntingdon train - arrived at 11.25am.
27.2	Special Train from Derby.
27.2	Request to Derby for postage and receipt stamps.
27.2	'Smokey chimneys' reported.
27.2	First dealing with St. Pancras - goods rates received from Derby for traffic to St. Pancras.
27.2	Dusters and whiting request to Derby.
27.2	Passenger fares' tables arrive.
1.3	One horse to Derby.
1.3	Cash box arrives from Leicester.
1.3	Fig.6 for ticket dating stamp, ticket punch, paper files and timetables request to Derby.
2.3	First ale arrives from Burton-on-Trent by rail.
3.3	Telegraph post removed.
3.3	Rate for granite from Mountsorrel requested from Derby.
4.3	11.25 train (from Leicester to Huntingdon).
4.3	First order from Thomas Smith (barley for Peterborough).
7.3	Poultry and eggs to London; one horse to Derby.
7.3	Toll gate charges (from Derby).
8.3	First pigs despatched (to Birmingham).
11.3	Revised passenger fares arrive.
11.3	Engine disabled (no details).
14.3	Request for 'measure forms' from Derby.
14.3	7.45am train (ex Cambridge) for Derby.
14.3	Request to Derby for cash as change.
15.3	Telegraphing trains from Derby.
16.3	T. Smith's grass seed request to Huntingdon.

16.3	Horse collar from Derby.
17.3	Horse collar from Derby.
17.3	Sack receipt book from Nottingham.
18.3	Circulars from Derby.
20.3	Engine derailed in station.
20.3	Horse collar from Derby.
22.3	Club contributions (the old health insurance scheme) to Derby- 2 shillings.
23.3	Party of 'Volunteers' to Derby (old equivalent of Territorials).
23.3	Another party of 'Volunteers'; free pass for drayman Claypole's wife etc.
23.3	Hand lamp to Derby for repairs.
23.3	Request to Derby for 'envelopes and memorandums'.
24.3	First monthly traffic returns sent to Derby.
24.3	First tickets sold for journeys to Brampton (Buckden) - ticket nos. 000 & 001.
24.3	Coal wagon No.184 from Pinxton,Derbyshire.
27.3	Rates received for roofing slates from Bangor, N. Wales (1st order of its kind).
28.3	Three desks and stools from Derby.
28.3	T. Smith described as a 'Merchant'.
29.3	Six hampers of meat despatched for Leicester. 'Special train' from Leicester.
31.3	Five tons of Guano arrive from Huntingdon.
31.3	Working timetable for excursions received from Derby.
3.4	Mr Bent sent one bag of potatoes to 'Graffham'.
4.4	Notice to announce single line working from Huntingdon to Cambridge.
5.4	T. Smith buys in 10 quarters of maize from St. Pancras.
6.4	Free pass for W. Partridge (porter).
7.4	12 files from Derby.
7.4	Mr Milligan received 'seed' (potatoes?) from Dumfries.
9.4	Special train from Derby.
11.4	Second recent shipment of pigs to Wellingborough.
14.4	Cattle plague report from Derby.
14.4	Order for T. Smith - granite from Ratby (Glenfield, Leics.).
16.4	First kilner of sugar to be delivered by train.
17.4	Bags of manure (20) from Huntingdon.
24.4	'Smokey chimneys' reported to Derby again.
24.4	Two hampers of wine (short weight) from Kettering, ordered by Mr Copland.
25.4	Plants for Horticultural Exhibition in London.
26.4	Delivery of sugar, damaged.
26.4	Cattle plague notified from Derby again.
27.4	Porter Partridge ill - reported to Derby. Sheep despatched for London.
27.4	Kimbolton Volunteers back from Derby.
29.4	More Kimbolton Volunteers back from Derby.
29.4	Lambs killed on the line.
29.4	Water closet broken.
1.5	3 wagons of cattle left for Kettering.
1.5	Another lamb killed on the line.

2.5	More cattle plague notification from Derby (cattle still being moved - see 1.5).
2.5	Shoeing bills to Derby.
3.5	Rate for transport of ale from Loughborough received.
3.5	Timetable of excursions received.
10.5	Two Volunteers from Cambridge.
10.5	List of stations with cattle dock facilities received.
15.5	Platelayers time sheets sent to Derby.
15.5	Porter Partridge's (further?) illness reported to Derby.
15.5	First reference to Duke of Manchester using station for goods.
20.5	Duke's Volunteers to Derby.
22.5	Second class passenger caught riding first class.
31.5	Porter Partridge's application for advance (of money? Probably due to illness and not being in receipt of a wage during this time).
1.6	Porter Flinder's cap arrives from Derby.
8.6	Special train bound for St. Ives.
8.6	Well dry.
13.6	Porter Doffern's cap arrives from Derby.
15.6	Bag for Tilbrook Church.
23.6	Well still dry.
24.6	Ellis & Co. bricks from Coalville.
29.6	Night trains.
29.6	Guard Portans' application for leave of absence.
5.7	Wagon off line; wagon off line again.
6.7	Wagon off line again; wagon off line again! (rotten drivers or permanent way staff).
6.7	Cleansing of cattle wagons (disinfecting due to cattle plague?).
8.7	Staff alterations.
10.7	Wagon off line yet again.
12.7	Further staff alterations. Account opened with Duke of Manchester.
25.7	T Smith's granite arrives from Ratby (Glenfield).
25.7	Rolling stock from Whitehaven & Furness Railway Co, and Whitehaven Junction Company.
31.7	Cotton cake delivered for T Smith.
3.8	Water delivered. (A bit of a drought?)
18.8	Wool for Leeds.
14.9	Mr Hensman's ale arrives from Burton on Trent.
16.9	Mr Golightly receives '2 crossings' from Sheffield.
26.9	Clay Cross Co. - lime from Clay Cross, Derbyshire.
26.9	Clay Cross Co. - lime from Ambergate. (Crich Quarry, now the home of the National Tram Museum, Derbys.)

Appendix Two

First Coal Deliveries to Kimbolton Station

21.2	Invoice. (Sent to Pinxton, East Derbyshire for coal.)
1.3	Mr Kinson's coal.
9.3	Mr Kinson's coal.
11.3	'Coal ground' order to Derby.
15.3	Order for coal to Mexborough, Yorkshire.
20.3	2 'B' coal trucks from Nether Birchwood Colliery, (Somercotes, East Derbyshire)
21.3	Two coal trucks sent to Cranford.
23.3	Three coal trucks from Derby.
23.3	Coal truck from Coalville.
27.4	Two coal trucks from NB. (Nether Birchwood?)
3.5	Coal from 'Ripley Gate to Kimbolton'. (Ripley is in East Derbyshire. 'Gate' may refer to original Ripley station on Pease Hill, Marehay, a suburb of Ripley.)
15.6	Coal from Coates Park Colliery. (Somercotes, Derbys.)
11.7	Coal from Mexborough.
25.7	Coal for use of station. (delivered from Derby.)
25.7	Coal from Coates Park Colliery.

Appendix Three

Details of the Engines Serving Kimbolton in 1869

Kirtley-designed locomotives - each class appears to have had five or six members allocated to work the line. New engines were added to the initial stock as trade expanded.

Class 2-2-2 built by Sharp Bros, Manchester

No.	Built	Rebuilt as 2-4-0	Broken up
41	11/1847	3/1862	8/1872
42	11/1847	7/1860	7/1875
44	12/1847	5/1861	7/1875
46	1/1848	1/1859	6/1873
47	1/1848	10/1861	2/1874
70	Class 2-4-0 built by Midland Railway Co., Derby		
88	12/1863	4/1888	
150	Class 2-4-0 built by Midland Railway Co., Derby		
153	7/1859	8/1873	
240	Class 0-6-0 (Standard Goods) built by R & W Hawthorn, Newcastle upon Tyne		
243	1851	6/1872	
246	3/1851	?	
247	3/1851	?	
248	3/1851	?	
256	9/1851	?	
259	1851	?	
240	Class 0-6-0 (Standard Goods) built by Mid. R'y, Derby		
322	1860 (as no. 203)	1873	1890 (renumbered to 322 in 1866)
480	Class 0-6-0 (Standard Goods) built by Mid. R'y Co., Derby		
323	1865 ('Special' use only)		11/1903
480	Class 0-6-0 (Standard Goods) built by Robert Stephenson & Co., Darlington		
480	1863	1881 & 1899	12/1932
481	1863	1879,1896,1911	4/1925
488	11/1863	1880 & 1896	
493	12/1863	1881,1897,1912	10/1925
499	12/1863	1880,1895,1909	1/1926
480	Class 0-6-0 built by Sharp, Stewart & Co., Manchester		
621	1867	1882,1900,1915	12/1930
623	1868	1883,1898,1917	11/1932
624	1868	1883,1902,1903,1912	11/1929
627	1868	1883,1889,1915	7/1925
628	1868	1882 & 1897	3/1925

Built by Mid. R'y, Derby

681	1868	1884 & 1900	4/1928
700	Class 0-6-0 built by Dubs & Co., Glasgow		
709	1869	1882,1898,1910,1917	9/1928
713	1869	1883 & 1898	11/1932
715	1869	1890,1902,1910,1913	12/1932
718	1869	1884,1900,1919	1928
719	1869	1882,1899,1923	11/1932

Built by Neilson & Co., Glasgow

721	1869	1885,1899,1922	12/1927

Appendix Four - Timetables

Passenger Timetable for Kimbolton in March 1866 (first month of operation)
(as extracted from the official Midland Railway timetable)

Weekdays Sundays

	am	pm	pm	pm	am	pm
Up (from Kettering)	9.11	12.7	3.27	7.30 -	10.41	8.26
Down (from Cambridge)	9.11	12.7	4.27	7.30 -	8.16	5.54

The timetable was mainly designed for trains to pass one another at Kimbolton Station. As can be seen in the extracts from the first log-book three additional trains passed through Kimbolton, from Leicester on their way to Huntingdon, at 11.25 am on February 24th, 26th and March 4th. Were they passenger specials or goods trains?

Daily (Mon-Sat) Passenger Timetable for 1870
   (as extracted from the Kimbolton Signal-box register)
For Wednesday March 16th
Up Trains (ex Kettering) Down Trains (ex Huntingdon)

	Due	Arrived	Departed	Due	Arrived	Departed
am	8.26	8.26	8.41	8.25	8.39	8.41
	11.48	11.47	11.50 pm	12.38	12.40	12.41
pm	3.31	3.40	3.50	3.32	3.32	3.50
	8.1	8.1	8.4	7.19	7.27	7.30

No Sunday passenger service

By 1870 the times of passenger trains arriving at Kimbolton had been changed totally, and, according to the signal-box register, the Sunday service had ceased.

Winter Goods Timetable for Week Thurs March 10 - Wed March 16 1870
Up Goods (ex Kettering) Down Goods (ex Huntingdon)

	Due	Arrived	Departed	Due	Arrived	Departed
Thurs	10.3	12.55	1.10	1.30	12.6	12.10 12.11
	4.48	4.49	4.50	1.50	2.5	2.20
	5.16	6.50	6.53	3.2	3.2	3.35
Fri	11.3	12.55	1.55	2.00	12.6	12.55 1.00
	4.48	5.15	5.35	1.50	2.5	2.20
	5.2	6.00	6.8	3.2	3.2	3.15
Sat	12.3	12.55	1.50	2.00	12.6	12.35 12.36
	4.48	4.45	5.00	1.50	2.5	2.15
	5.8	6.15	6.20	3.2	3.50	4.5
Sun	13.3	No Goods		12.6	12.25	12.26

	Due	Arrived	Departed		Due	Arrived	Departed
Mon	14.3	No train logged		12.6	12.25	12.26	
	4.48	5.5	5.20	1.50	2.20	2.40	
	5.8	5.40	5.45	7.27	7.20	7.30	
Tues	15.3	12.55	1.30	1.35	12.6	12.38 12.40	
	4.48	4.45	5.5	1.50	4.10	4.50	
	5.8	8.25	8.53	3.2	3.10	3.35	
Wed	16.3	12.55	12.30	1.00	12.6	12.50 12.51	
	4.48	5.10	5.30	1.15	2.32	2.50	
	5.8	6.3	6.14	3.2	3.5	3.35	

Average length of stay = 12.9 mins. = 13.5 mins.
For the first nine minutes past the hour the 'nought' was always omitted - e.g. 3.05 as 3.5
Summer Goods Timetable for Week Mon Aug 1 - Sun Aug 7 1870
Up Goods Down Goods

	Due	Arrived	Departed	Due	Arrived	Departed
Mon Aug 1	12.36	12.35	12.45	12.31	12.25	12.40
	4.48	4.57	5.10	1.50	2.5	2.10
	5.8	5.20	5.30	3.2	2.10	2.35
Tues Aug 2	12.36	1.00	1.5	12.31	12.30	1.00
	4.48	4.48	5.00	1.50	2.5	2.20
	5.8	5.25	5.35	2.18	2.20	2.35
Wed Aug 3	12.31	12.5	12.50	12.36	12.50	12.50
	4.48	4.47	5.00	1.50	2.10	2.30
	5.8	6.40	6.45	2.18	2.20	2.25
Thur Aug 4	12.36	12.35	12.37	12.36	12.34	12.45
	2.18	2.10	2.30	1.50	2.30	2.45
	4.48	4.45	5.30	5.8	5.35	5.45
Fri Aug 5	12.36	12.35	12.55	12.36	12.50	12.52
	4.48	4.52	5.5	1.50	2.10	2.30
	5.8	5.20	5.40	2.18	2.20	2.35
Sat Aug 6	4.48	5.00	5.10	1.50	2.5	2.15
Sun Aug 7	5.8	5.25	5.35	12.36	12.50	12.55
	7.15	7.15	7.30			

Average length of stay = 14.8 mins. = 12.4 mins.

Appendix Five

Imperial to Metric Conversions

Liquids

1.75 pints = 1 litre
8 pints = 1 gallon
1 gallon = 4.5 litres

Areas

2.5 acres = 1 hectare
640 acres = 250 hectares = 1 square mile

Weights

2240 pounds (lbs) = 1 ton
2205 pounds = 1 (metric) tonne
112 pounds = 1 hundredweight (cwt.)
1 quarter = 28 pounds = 12.75 kilograms
14 pounds = 1 stone Distance
2.2 pounds = 1 kilogram 1 mile = 8 furlongs

Money (metrication in February 1971)

1p = 2.4 old pennies (d)
100p = 240 pennies = £1
5p = 12 pennies = 1 shilling (s)
20 shillings = £1

Appendix Six

Sampled Details of "Goods Received" Nov'70-Nov'71

Date	From	Consignee	Abode	Weight/Nos.	Carter
Slag					
4.1	Wellingboro'	Denton	Swineshead	12t	Wiggins X
4.2	"	Manns	Spaldwick	9t 19cwt	R. Carter
7.8	Thrapstone	Golightly	Kimbolton	26t 10c	W. Brunning
30.9	Wellingboro'	Manns	"	31t 6c	G. Hall X

Annual Total: 718 tons 5cwt.

Granite					
27.4	Bardon Hill	Ellis & Ev.	Kimbolton	19t 7c	J. Wiggins X
13.6	Glenfield	Denton	Swineshead	6t 3c	Denton
2.8	Mountsorrel	Pattison	Kimbolton	32t	G. Farr

Annual Total: 463 tons 7cwt.

Fertilizer					
11.2	Huntingdon	Smith	Tilbrook	5t	?
18.2	Birkenhead	T. Smith	"	10t 11c-guano	?
22.2	Birmingham	John Mason	Brington	1t 10c-manure	Mason
1.3	Bramford	S.Pashler	Catworth	2t coprolite	Fred Locks
6.3	Blackwall	J. Wilson	Kimbolton	2t manure	Collins
6.3	London	Smith	Tilbrook	2t "	"
24.3	Huntingdon	Pashler	Molesworth	2t "	Bowyer X

Annual Totals: Manure-87t; Coprolite-32t; Guano-15t 11cwt.

Animal Feed					**Feed**
3.11	Huntingdon	Chapman	Wornditch	2t	Linseed Cake
19.11	London	Smith	Tilbrook	4t	Maize
23.11	Thrapstone	Spiller	Kimbolton	2t	Palm Nut Meal
29.11	Hull	Smith	Tilbrook	5t	Cotton Cake
21.12	Huntingdon	Spicer	Kimbolton	2t	Hog Meal
1.2	"	Measures	Catworth	1t	Linseed Cake
22.2	"	Pashler	"	2t	"
3.4	Waterloo(Liv'l)	Smith	Tilbrook	3t	"
11.4	London	"	"	14t 10c	Tares
14.4	"	"	"	2t	Locust Beans
25.4	Canada	"	Kimbolton	3t	Cotton Cake
26.5	K. Lynn	D. Cooper	Spaldwick	2t	Oats
11.6	Huntingdon	Smith	Tilbrook	2t 10c	Barley
16.8	Blackwall	Willson	Kimbolton	2t 1c 2q	Cotton Cake
30.9	Victoria Docks	Smith	Tilbrook	5t	Maize
11.10	St. Pancras	"	"	18t 6c 2q	Barley

Annual Totals: Linseed Cake-204tons   Maize -155tons   Locust Beans - 5tons
                     Cotton Cake -100 "   Oats -124 "   Meal   - 31 "
                     Cakes   - 81 "   Barley - 70 "   Peas   - 16 "
                     Tares   - 21 "   Wheat - 22 "   Annual Total - 829 tons

Seeds

Date	Origin	Consignee	Destination	Weight	Goods
28.3	Huntingdon	Smith	"	10c 2q 14lb	20sacks grass seed
6.4	"	"	"	4t	Peas
12.7	"	"	"	2t	Rape Seed

Pollards

Date	Origin	Consignee	Destination	Weight	
22.12	Huntingdon	Smith	Tilbrook	2t	
5.1	"	Spicer	Kimbolton	2t	
5.5	"	Chapman	Wornditch	2t	

Annual Total - 35t 1cwt.

Wine

Date	Origin	Consignee	Destination	Weight	Goods
20.12	London	Smith	Tilbrook	1q 23lb	1 Case
23.1	"	Bell	Brington	1c	"
14.7	Cambridge	Holmes	Catworth	3q 18lb	"

Ale, Stout, Spirits & Tobacco

Date	Origin	Consignee	Destination	Weight	Goods
16.12	Wellingboro'	Pashler	Catworth	2c	1 Kilner Ale
21.12	St. Pancras	B. Clarke	Kimbolton	2q	1 Box Tobacco

(the only order in the year, rail borne)

Date	Origin	Consignee	Destination	Weight	Goods
14.2	Thrapstone	Campion	Dean	1c	1 Firkin Ale
16.5	Huntingdon	Clark	Kimbolton Station		3 Jars Spirits
29.5	Wellingboro'	Pashler	Molesworth	2c	1 Kilner Stout
5.10	Burton-on-Trent	Watson	Kimbolton	1c 3q 20lb	1 Kilner Ale

Annual Totals- Firkins- 13 : Kilners- 17

Cheese

Date	Origin	Consignee	Destination	Weight	Goods
2.8	Huntingdon	Hollis	Catworth	2q 14lb	2 Boxes

Flour

Date	Origin	Consignee	Destination	Weight	Goods
5.1	St. Ives	Smith	Tilbrook	2c 2q	1 Sack
13.6	Huntingdon	"	"	5c	2 Sacks

Confectionery

Date	Origin	Consignee	Destination	Weight	Goods
23.9	Leicester	Jebbs	Catworth	1c 1q 7lb	1 Chest

Farm Animals-Arrivals

Date	Origin	Consignee	Destination	Animals	Goods
19.12	St. Ives	Dickens	Catworth	Geese	2 Hoppers(!)
30.12	Kettering	Blackwell	Kimbolton	2 Beast	
23.1	Huntingdon	Smith	Tilbrook	15 Sheep	
7.8	St. Ives	Spicer	Kimbolton	10 Pigs	

Annual Arrivals: Beast- 40; Sheep- 130; Pigs- 18; Geese

Agricultural Equipment

7.11	St. Ives	Smith	Tilbrook	Turnip Cutter, Hole & Hook, Skip, Chaff Cutter
16.12	Thrapstone	Holmes	Catworth	1 Pulper
15.4	Bedford	Gambrill	Tilbrook	Casting
8.6	"	Holmes	Catworth	2 Harrows : Pole
26.6	Thrapstone	Golightly	Kimbolton	2t Fencing
25.9	London	Ratcliffe	Leighton	1 Cultivator, 4 Bundles Shares
23.10	St. Ives	Smith	Tilbrook	Cake Breaker, Hawk Wrench, 1 Wheel

Soap

17.3	Wakefield	Smith	Catworth	5c 1q	5 Boxes

Furniture

15.11	Huntingdon	Chattell	Leighton	3c 1q 6lb	1 Lot
13.3	London	Duke of Man.	Kimbolton	1t 4lb	50 Packages

Coal

20.5	Thrapstone	Holmes	Catworth	3t 15c	1 Truck

Oil & Grease

14.12	London	Giddings	Kimbolton	5c 2q 8lb	2 Barrels Oil
18.9	Derby	Spriggs	"		1 Cask Grease

Clothes

30.1	London	Brown	Catworth	1q	1 Bundle
21.10	Raunds	Smith	Catworth	2q 26lb	"
4.11	"	Brown	Dean	"	"

Annual Orders: 69 Bundles (19.5cwt). Main Dealers:-

Brown - 32 Dean & Catworth: Whitney - 5 Catworth
T H Smith - 10 Tilbrook : Abbott - 3 Old Weston: Hewitt - 3 Catworth

Ropes, String & Sheets

15.3	Burton	Agent	Kimbolton	15 Midland Sheets
17.5	London	Agent	Kimbolton	2 Ropes
21.9	Trent Junction	Spriggs	"	1 Bundle Strings
25.9	"	"	"	10 Midland Sheets

Annual Total of Sheets- 75 all delivered free

Building Materials & Ironmongery

22.2	Derby	Golightly	Kimbolton	2t 10c	Bolts & Keys
3.10	Huntingdon	Bent	Melchbourne		3 boxes Glass, 3 Packages Wood, 1 Box Glass
14.10	Peterboro'	Lovell	Dean	3t 15c	Deals & Scantling
24.10	London	Myres & Son	Kimbolton		10 Window Frames, 2 Fres. Windings,200 Gals Iron Tiles 1 Package Bowls

Iron Ore

24.6	Wellingboro'	Denton	Swineshead	11t 6c	2 Trucks
27.7	"	Mann	Brampton	25t 3c	4 Trucks

Pipes

17.3	Leeds	Martyn	Pertenhall	2t 10c	640 pipes
31.5	Woodville	Love	Kimbolton	7t 10c	

Annual Total - 14 tons 16 cwt.

Duke of Manchester's Orders

17.11	Belfast	Kimbolton	4c 3q	9 Plates, 2 Troughs
30.11	"	"	12c	Iron

Kimbolton Gas Company

15.4	Gt. Bridge	Kimbolton	3t 10c	Iron

Empty Sacks

11.11	Trent Junction	Agent	Kimbolton	50 Bundles
12.11	Huntingdon	Spicer	"	40 "
19.11	Wellingboro'	Wallis	Park Farm	2 "
31.1	Kettering	Milligan	Dean	4 "
7.2	Huntingdon	Smith	Tilbrook	8 "

Annual Totals- 1208 Bundles at 1 cwt. each. 135 Orders.

Main Orderers: Goods Agent - 640; T H Smith - 159; Spicer - 90;
Milligan - 49; Wilson - 36; Hollis - 20; Others - 213

Origins of Empty Sacks:-		
Trent Junction	- 17 orders	- 640 bundles
Huntingdon	- 25 "	- 213 "
Wellingboro'	- 28 "	- 86 "
Birmingham	- 13 "	- 58 "
St. Ives	- 6 "	- 26 "
Atherstone	- 7 "	- 21 "
Kettering	- 6 "	- 21 "

Baskets

20.3	Huntingdon	Chapman	Wornditch	4	Bundles Baskets
13.6	Raunds	Dorrington	Leighton	8	" "
4.8	Cambridge	Smith	Tilbrook	1	" "

Annual Total - 20

INDEX

INDEX

P. F. 70
R 2—10.000—11.08.

Midland Railway.

KIMBOLTON